AF522354

RURAL DEVELOPMENT IN INDIA

RURAL DEVELOPMENT IN INDIA

By

B. K. Sahu

ANMOL PUBLICATIONS PVT. LTD.

NEW DELHI - 110 002 (INDIA)

ANMOL PUBLICATIONS PVT. LTD.
4374/4B, Ansari Road, Daryaganj
New Delhi - 110 002
Ph.: 23261597, 23278000
Visit us at: www.anmolpublications.com

Rural Development in India
© Author
First Edition, 2003

ISBN 81-261-1493-2

[All rights reserved. No part of this publication may be reproduced, stored in a retrieval system or transmitted, in any form or by any means, mechanical, photocopying, recording or otherwise, without prior written permission of the publisher.]

PRINTED IN INDIA

Published by J.L. Kumar for Anmol Publications Pvt. Ltd., New Delhi - 110 002 and Printed at Tarun Offset Press, Delhi.

CONTENTS

PREFACE

'Rural Development' encompasses all sectors of rural life. In its widest sense it implies development of every aspect of rural life. The basic objective of rural development is to organise, develop and utilise the available resources in such a manner that the entire population dependent on these resources has an equitable opportunity to meet as a minimum, its basic needs.

The experiences of past five decades of planning have proved beyond doubt that development of rural sector provides the key to the development and growth of our economy. Over the years a number of programmes have been implemented in the rural areas for achievement of full employment, eradication of poverty, provision of basic necessities, increase productivity of rural economic sectors and infrastructural development. Improvement of the socio-economic conditions of the weaker sections in the rural areas has been receiving considerable attention of the planners, policy makers, researchers and development agencies. The achievement of growth with social justice is being emphasized in the planning and development strategies. Attempts are made to eliminate the inherent maladies and the vicious circle existing in rural areas, to maximize the desired goals of development through a number of programmes. In order to improve the effectiveness of these programmes, management inputs have been identified to be one of the major variables. The programme management tasks is being performed by a number of Institutions/organisations working in the rural areas.

This book highlights the socio-economic condition of the country. The plan approaches for rural development in India is also received due importance in this book. In the process of planned economic development, the developments of rural economic activities have been received utmost attention. In this respect a number of rural development programmes have also been implemented in our country. A humble attempt is made, to analyse about 25 (Twenty Five) important rural development Programmes that has been implemented in our country in different periods. The success of rural development programmes depends upon the success of the project cycle such as, Identification, Formulation, Appraisal, Implementation, Monitoring and Evaluation. In order to carry out such activities a viable and healthy institution is required to operate in the rural scenario. In this connection, to support the rural development programmes there exists a number of institutions viz. Administrative setup, Panchayati Raj Institutions, Rural Credit Institutions. This book also throws light about the structure, organisation and functioning of these rural Institutions. Besides some photographs of rural areas (Orissa, Chhatisgarh, and Assam) will give a little idea about the rural India.

This book also highlights some common problems that has been encountered while implementing the different rural development programmes, and appropriate suggestions to overcome the same.

At the end a select and comprehensive bibliography of selected readings on rural development is provided. I hope, this will be helpful to the persons engaged and interested in the rural development of India.

This book perhaps, is the first attempt in viewing rural economy as a significant segment of country's economic structure. This book highlights the important rural development programmes, is the unique part of this study.

My debt to those who have helped me in one way or other. While I take this opportunity to thank all of them; they are too numerous to mention individually in a brief preface.

I express my debt of gratitude to my parents, Father, Ishwar Chandra Sahu and Mother Bari Sahu for generating in me a parental interest in higher studies. I will be failing in my duty if I do not mention here the tremendous cooperation I have received from my wife Mamata in the completion of this work. I also thankful to my friends and well wishers for their timely and valuable assistance at the time of requirement.

I offer my thanks to Kripal D. Joshi, Production Manager, M/s. Anmol Publications Pvt. Ltd., New Delhi, for promptly responding to my request for printing and publishing the book.

—B.K. Sahu

1
INTRODUCTION

THE COUNTRY

India is the seventh largest country in the world. It is well marked off from the rest of Asia by mountains and seas, which give the country a distinct geographical unity. Bounded by the great Himalayas in the North, it stretches southwards and at the tropic of cancer, tapers off into the Indian Ocean between the Bay of Bengal on the east and the Arabian Sea on the west. The country is lying entirely in the northern hemisphere, the main land extends between latitudes $8^{0}4'$ and $37^{0}6'$ north and longitudes $68^{0}7'$ and $97^{0}25'$ east and measures about 2,933 km from east to west between the extreme longitudes. It has a land frontier of about 15.2 thousand kms and a coastline of about 6.1 thousand kms.

Geographical Structure

The geographical region of the country is broadly grouped into three well-defined regions i.e., (i) The Himalayas (ii) the Indo-Grangetic Plains and (iii) the ancient penisular shield.

The Himalayan mountain belt to the north and the naga-lushai mountains in the east are regions of mountain building movement. In a series of mountain building movements commencing about seven crore years ago, the sediments and the basements of rocks in various configurations rose to great heights.

The Indo-Gangetic plains are a great alluvial tract that separates the Himalayas from the peninsula to the south. The deposits of the tracts belong to the latest chapter of the earth's history and conceal beneath them the southern fringes of the Himalayan formations and the northern fringes of the peninsular formations.

The peninsula is a region of relative stability and rare seismic disturbances. Highly metamorphosed rocks of the earliest periods occur over more than half of its area the rest being covered by the coal bearing Gondwana formations and later sediments and lava flows belonging to the Deccan trap formation.

Geographical Features

The main land comprises four well-defined regions, namely, the great mountain zone, plains of the Ganga and the Indus, the desert region and the southern peninsula.

The Himalayas comprise three almost parallel ranges interspersed with large plateau and valleys some of which like the Kashmir and Kulu Valleys are fertile, extensive and of great science beauty. Some of the highest peaks in the world are found in these ranges. The mountain wall extends over a distance of about 2.4 thousand kms with a varying depth of 240 to 320 Km. In the east between India and Burma and India and Bangladesh the hill ranges are much lower. The Garo, Khasi, Jaintia and Naga hills running almost east-west join the Chain of the mizo and Arakan hills running north-south.

Plains of the Ganga and the Indus, about 2.4 thousand Kms long and the basins of three distinct river systems, the Indus, the Ganga and the Brahmaputra, form 240 to 320 Kms broad. They are one of the world's greatest stretches of flat alluvium and also one of the most densely populated areas on earth.

The desert region can be divided into two parts—the great desert and the little desert. The great desert extends from the edge of the Rann of Kuchchh beyond the Luni River between Jaisalmer and Jodhpur up to the northern wastes.

The peninsular plateau is marked off from the plains of the Ganga and the Indus by a mass of mountain and hill ranges varying from 460 to 1220 meters in height. Prominent among these are the Aravalli, Vindhya, Satpura, Maikala and Ajanta. The peninsula is flanked on one side by the Eastern Ghats, where the average elevation is about 610 metres and on the other by the Western Ghats. The Southern point of the plateau is formed by the Nilgiri hills where the Eastern Ghats and Western Ghats meet.

Climate

The climate of India may be broadly described as tropical monsoon type. There are four seasons in India (i) winter season (January - February) (ii) Hot weather season, summer (March-May) (iii) rainy reason, Southwestern monsoon period (June-September) and (iv) Post-monsoon period in the Southern peninsula (October-December). In India, rainfall is erratic and ill distributed. Cherrapunji gets 11, 419 mm of annual rainfall the highest in the country. In contrast, Rajasthan, Kachchh and the high Ladakh plateau of Kashmir extending westward to Gilgit are regions of low precipitation. They have a yearly rainfall of between 100 mm and 500 mm. The change in environmental situation is reported to have positive effect on the climatic conditions of the country. Due to these, the average rainfall of the Cherrpunji is declining whereas, the state Rajasthan experiencing floods.

Demography

In terms of population, India is the second largest country in the world next only to China. It accounts for 15.6 per cent of the world population. According to 1991 census, the population of India is 846 million. Uttar Pradesh is the most populous state of India and the population of Haryana is the smallest among the major states. The distribution of male and female population was stood at 52 per cent and 48 per cent respectively. The ratio of females per 1000 male is 929 in 1991 census. The Density of population is 267 persons per square kilometer. According to 1991 census 74.3 per cent of the total population live in rural areas and the remaining 25.7 per cent in urban areas of the country. It is thus observed that, India is predominated by rural population. The rural populations generally live in about 576 thousand villages of the country.

The distribution of scheduled caste and Scheduled Tribe population is India in 16.5 per cent and 8.1 per cent respectively to the total population.

Work force

Out of the total population, workers constitute about 37.5 per cent. The distribution of work force is 79.2 per cent and 20.8 per cent respectively for rural and urban areas in the country. Among the total male workers 75.1 per cent were employed in rural areas and the remaining 24.9 per cent were in the urban areas. Among the female workers, the rural workers accounted for about 89.2 per cent and urban workers at 10.8 per cent. Obviously, the percentage of total workers in the rural areas among the total workers in the country is 79.2 per cent while the percentage of population living in the rural areas is 74.3 per cent. Sex-wise, 75.1 per cent of the male workers and 89.2 per cent of the female workers in the country have been enumerated in rural areas whereas 73.81 per cent of the male population and 74.8 per cent of the female population lived in rural areas. The distribution of work force in rural areas of the country shows that, there are 35.8 per cent main workers and 4.3 per cent marginal workers. The distribution of rural main workers shows that 48.2 per cent are cultivators, 32.2

Generally poverty can be classified into two such as; (i) Absolute Poverty (ii) Relative Poverty

Absolute Poverty: This implies a person's lack of access to objectively determined, reasonable adequate quantities of goods and services to satisfy his/her material and non-material Basic needs.

Relative Poverty: This means that a person's access to the basic needs of life is relatively lower as compared to some reference group of people.

per cent are agricultural labourers, 2.2 per cent workers employed in household industries and the remaining 17.4 per cent workers in rural areas reported to be engaged in other activities in rural economy, more particularly in service sectors.

Unemployment

The planning commission has prepared estimates of unemployment by applying the rates of unemployment as obtained from NSS data to the projected population. The backlog of unemployment for planning process in the beginning of Eighth plan (1990-95) was 28 million. The new entrants to the labour force during the plant period was estimated to be 37 million, bringing the total to about 65 million. It was also estimated that the new entrants to the labour force during the Ninth plan (1997-2002) would be about 41 million. This volume of unemployment would be about 106 millions during the Ninth Plan period.

The people of India generally employed in organized sector and unorganized sector. The organized sector is the hub of the Indian economy and so it tends to loom large in public imagination. However, it accounts for only about 13 per cent of our total labour force. On the other hand, the unorganized sector accounts for the remaining 87 per cent covering a large part of agricultural workers, and those engaged in small and cottage industry, trade, professional services etc. The entire unorganized segment falls within the private sector.

POVERTY

Poverty can be defined as a social phenomenon in which a section of the society is enables to fulfill even its basic necessities of life. When a substantial segment of a society is said to be plagued with mass poverty. The countries of the Third World exhibit invariably the existence of mass poverty, although pockets of poverty exist even in the developed countries of Europe and America. Poverty in economic literature is of two types, i.e; the absolute and the relative. In the absolute standard, the minimum physical quantities of cereals pulses, milk, butter etc. are determined for subsistence level and then the price quotations convert into monetary terms the physical quantities. Aggregating all the quantities included, a figure expressing per capita consumer expenditure is determined. The population whose level of income is below the figure is considered to be below poverty line. According to the relative standard, income distribution of the population in different fractile groups is estimated and a comparison of the standard of living of the top 5 to 10 per cent with the bottom 5 to 10 per cent of the population reflects the relative standardards of poverty. In India the incidence of poverty is commonly determined by adopting the absolute standards methods.

In India, about 35.9 per cent of the total population reported to be live below poverty line in 1993 1994. The incidence of rural and urban population living below poverty line is 37.3 per cent and 32.4 per cent respectively, in India. The percentage of population below poverty line in Bihar is highest in the country at 54.6 per cent and least in Punjab at 11.8 per cent in the year under observation. It is also observed that Bihar stood first with 58.2 per cent and Goa the last with 5.3 per cent of the rural population live below poverty line. In Madhya Pradesh about 48.3 per cent of the urban population live below the poverty line, which is highest in the country. Taking the high incidence of poverty in India into consideration it is required more positive steps to eradicate poverty at a faster rate.

Agriculture

The agricultural sector contributes nearly 8 per cent of the national Income, provides livelihood to about two-third of the population, supplies the bulk of wage goods required by the non-agricultural sector and raw materials for a large section of industry. It also provides a substantial portion of the Country's exports, Transport. Marketing, Processing and other aspects of agricultural production and utilization have also a strong bearing on the national economy.

In India the net area available for crop agriculture is about 165 million hectares, accounted for about 50 per cent to the total geographical area of the country. The percentage of net area shown to total area is stood at 46.6 per cent in 1993-94. The distribution of farmers according to land holdings shows that about 13 per cent of the land is hold away by 58 per cent Marginal Farmers, 16 per cent of land by 18 per cent small farmers, 22 per cent of land by 14 per cent of Semi-medium farmers, 29 per cent of land by 8 per cent medium farmers and the remaining 20 per cent of land by only 2 per cent large farmers. The fragmentation of holding upon inheritance among the successors as also the distribution of acquired surplus land among the weaker lots of farming community, increases the number of marginal and small land holdings in the country. This smallholding causes low percapita productivity and existence of poverty among marginal and small farmers.

Water is indispensable to agricultural production. The important source of water in our country is rainfall; nearly two-third of agricultural land is in rain fed areas. The remaining one-third of the area is prone to vagaries of monsoon like, droughts, and floods. In India 35 per cent of the net cropped area was irrigated by artificial irrigation sources like canals, wells, tube-wells, tanks and other sources. After 50 years of planned economic development the country failed to attain substantial level of irrigation facilities. Needless to add that, if higher production growth targets in agriculture are to be attained then increasing the use of available irrigation potential and extension of the facility over larger cropped land would have to be attended to with due urgency. It is noteworthy that the share of our country to total irrigated land in the world has stood at 19.4 per cent.

The farmers of India generally use wooden or Iron ploughs for the cultivation of land. The use of power tillers and tractors is less. In the country about 12 Lakh tractors are in operation. The share of the country to world tractors in use was 4.6 per cent according 1995.

The consumption of chemical fertilizer is an essential input for agricultural development. It is observed that Indian farmer uses 14 million tonnes chemical fertilizers on 1995-96 as against

131 million tonnes in the world level use. The percentage share of fertilizers used in India to World is about 10.7 per cent.

The important crops grown in India are, Rice (Paddy), Wheat, Cereals, Potatoes, Groundnuts, Rapeseeds, Coffee, Sugarcane, Tea, Jute and Cotton etc. It is also observed that more than 50 per cent of the Jutes produced in World produced in India.

ALLIED ACTIVITIES

Allied activities assume crucial importance in the rural economy is more than one aspect. They play a very important role in bringing about a balance in the production system and utilization of resources, in smoothening the income flows between seasons in ensuring participation of people with no or inadequate land resources in productive activities and bringing about a balance in nutritive value of firm products. The land as a basis of production system is either not available for number of people or is available in very adequate quantity. Therefore, crop husbandry cannot be looked upon as a source of self-employment and income for a substantial proportion of the population in the rural areas. For these sections of people i.e; landless labourers and Marginal farmers, allied activities can provide a source of gainful self-employment. The allied activities such as dairy, sheep and goat husbandry, piggery, poultry and fishery etc. have a very important role to play in stabilising the rural economy of the rural people. India is the top of the world having one-sixth of the livestock population - less than one fifth of cattle, half of the buffaloes, and over one-fifth of goats and sheeps. Despite of its international importance, it contributes only 20 per cent of the gross value of output from agriculture. Whereas this is more than 50 per cent in advanced countries of the world.

INDUSTRIALIZATION

Industrialization has a major role to play in the economic development of the under developed countries. The gap in percapita incomes between the developed and underdeveloped countries is largely reflected in the separate in the structure of their economies; the former are largely industrial economies, while in the latter production is confined predominantly to agriculture. India is a country of rural dominant economy depends mostly on agriculture, small and rural industries, small business and retail trade for her development. In order to attain rural industrialisation the adoption of labour-intensive technology in labour abundant areas and capital-intensive technology in labour-scarce economies only attacks the peripheral problem in rural economies. Creation of employment opportunities in urban sector by developing large-scale industrial base seems to have failed to attract the rural masses in the country. It is therefore, felt necessary to create such opportunity in the rural sector. Moreover, creation of job opportunities does not need as much investment in this rural industrial sector as in the large-scale sector. As against this background, the planners and policy makers have been laid more emphasis on the development of small and rural industries. It is observed that, the share of small industries in the entire factory sector in terms of number of units has been high annual 90 per cent but in employment, it accounts for around 35 per cent on the other hand it accounts for about a fourth in gross output and one-fifth of the value added in the entire factory sector. The traditional village industries also exist in India. One of the special characteristics of the traditional village industries is that they cannot provide fulltime employment to workers, but instead can provide only subsidiary or part-time employment opportunities to agricultural labourers and artisans. Among traditional village industries, handicrafts possess the highest labour productivity; besides, handicrafts make a significant contribution to earning foreign exchange for the country. Under these circumstances, active encouragement of handicrafts is required in priority basis. It is also evident that, labourers and artisans living below the poverty line, while modern small industries can provide a good source of living largely carry on traditional village and small industries. Hence, if with an expansion of employment, the number of persons living below the poverty line has also to be reduced, and then a rapid and much larger expansion of the modern small sector will have to be planned. However, the important sectors of the rural industries are, Khadi Cloth, Handlooms, Sericulture, Handicrafts, Coir industry, Small-scale industries, Power looms and Village industries.

INFRASTRUCTURE

The prosperity of a country depends directly upon the development of agriculture and industry. Agricultural development however, requires power, credit, transport facilities on the other hand industrial development requires, Machinery, Equipment Technically sound manpower, Appropriate Management, Energy, Banking facilities, Transport services and Communication facilities etc. All these facilities and services constitute collectively the infrastructure of an economy and the development and expansion of these facilities are an essential condition for attaining agricultural and industrial development in a country. However Infrastructure facilities often referred to as economic and social overheads like; (i) Energy (ii) Transport (iii) Communications (iv) Banking, Finance and Insurance (v) Science and Technology and (vi) Social overheads.

(1) **Energy**: Energy is an essential input of all productive economic activity. The main source of energy in rural areas are Fuel wood, Agricultural wastes, Animal dung as the traditional and non-commercial energies, coal, electricity, oil and gas are the non-traditional commercial energy available in the rural areas of the country. Taking the economic condition of the rural areas, the rural people mostly depend upon the traditional and non-commercial energy sources to meet their demands. In the course of time, these sources are declining rapidly. As against this background, the planners and policy makers laid more emphasis on the production of fuel woods through the adoption of social forestry in the rural areas of the country. In the context of rural electrification, about 86 per cent of the total villages in India are electrified. The states like Andhra Pradesh, Goa, Haryana, Himachal Pradesh, Kerala, Punjab, Tamilnadu and

Tripura attained cent per cent in connection with rural electrification. The states like Meghalaya, Uttarpradesh, Bihar and Orissa are lagging behind the national percentage.

(2) **Transport:** India is essentially an agrarian and rural based country, and roads constitute a critical element in the transportation. Road construction and maintenance generate sizeable employment opportunities. This also helps the rural people to a great extent for transportation of goods and human resources. The rural road network now connects about 70 per cent of the villages in India. But the percentage of villages connected with all weather roads has stood at only 48 per cent. This requires special attention by planners and policy maker while preparing programmes for rural development.

(3) **Communications:** The Communication system comprises posts, Telegraphs, Tele communication system, Broadcasting, Television and Information services. The postal network has been expanded throughout the country and in recent years, with special emphasis on the rural, hilly and tribal areas. In India there are 16 post offices serving one lakh population. The coverage of postal network is more in smaller and underdeveloped states like Mizoram, Himachal Pradesh, Sikkim and Manipur. Whereas the network is comparatively low in other developed and bigger states. The growth of Telecommunications is directly related to and woven with the growth of technologies in other sectors like the electronics, satellite communication, broadcasting network etc. It is to note here that there are 1.36 lakh rural post offices in India. The rural population per post office is reported to be about 5.7 thousand and area served by a post office was 21.5 square kilometers. There are about 17 thousand Telephone Exchanges served in rural areas of the country. Besides, there are 1.86 lakh public telephones exist in rural India on 1996.

(4) Credit Institutions

The credit requirement of the rural economic sectors generally met by two sources, i.e; Non-Institutional and institutional. The non-institutional credit agencies comprise money lenders, indigenous bankers, landlords, traders and commissioning agents, friends and relatives etc. They play an important role in dispensing credit in rural areas. About 40 per cent of the total rural credit requirement is met by non-institutional sources. The Institutional Credit, at present is provided by agencies like, co-operative banks, commercial banks and Regional Rural banks. National Bank For Agriculture & Rural Development (NABARD) is the apex institution for these institutional agencies. Besides, over the years an integrated structure of financial institutions has been evolved for providing term finance and other assistance to industrial sector. They comprise of IDBI, IFCI, ICICI, and SIDBI etc. The investment institutions comprise UTI, LIC, GIC also indirectly contribute towards the rural credit needs. Besides, there is also a network of state level institutions the SFCs and SIDCs. In India their exists the State Bank of India its Associated Banks (7) and 19 Nationalised banks bringing the total public sector bank to 27. They are directed to advance credit up to 40 per cent of the total bank credit to the priority sector. The priority sector in India comprises of agriculture, Small-scale Industry, Transport operators, retail trade and small business, professional and self-employed, housing loan to weaker sections and education. It is also evident that within the priority sector, agriculture continued to account for the maximum share of advances at about 18 per cent. However, there are 35.3 thousand rural branches accounted for about 58 per cent of the total bank branch network. The population per bank branch is stood at 11 thousand. Despite of importance on opening of rural braches, the rural people are inadequately served with commercial banks. The population per bank branch should reduce in such a way that the rural people will feel comfortable. The total priority sector advance was stood at Rs 99,507 crores on 1998. This is about 33.5 per cent of the total bank credit. The volume of priority sector advance is increasing but the percentage share to the total bank credit declining steadily. This situation arised due to ongoing economic reforms as well as banking sector reforms. Out of total priority sector advance, about 35.1 per cent credit was advanced to agricultural sector,

43.7 per cent to small-scale industries, and remaining 21.2 per cent to other priority sector.

The second important source of institutional finance is Regional Rural Banks. These banks were introduced to cater into the credit needs of the rural people. They were started functioning since 1976 in India. There are 196 Regional Rural Banks in India according to 1996. Over the period of twenty years they covered about 427 districts of the country, with the branch network of about 14.5 thousand. The total deposits mobilised by the RRBs was stood at Rs 14,188 crores ad the total loans and advances reached at Rs 7505 crores.

The last important source of institutional credit in the rural areas is co-operatives. Co-operatives, in our country treated as important instrument of rural development. At the primary level there are, Primary Agricultural Credit Societies, Farmers Service Societies, Primary Co-operative Banks, Primary non-agricultural credit societies and Primary Land Development Banks operating to serve rural people/areas of the country. At the secondary or middle level there are, Central Co-operative Banks and Central Land Development Banks act as a link between primary co-operatives and higher co-operatives operated/instituted at the State level. These are State Co-operative Banks and State Land Development Banks. It is revealed from the available data that, there are, 4.10 lakh co-operative societies serving rural population of the country. The total membership of these societies is stood at 1978 lakh during the year 1995-96. Furthermore, the co-operative network is highest in Maharastra, where there exist about 20 thousand Primary Agricultural Credit Societies. Whereas, only 35 PACs are functioning in Sikkim.

National Bank for Agriculture and Rural Development (NABARD) is the apex institution for these Institutional Credit Agencies. It provides finance and re-finance facilities to the institutional credit agencies operating at rural areas of the country. The important purposes for which NABARD advance finance/re-finance facilities are, Minor irrigation, Land Development, farm mechanism, plantation, Horticulture,

Poultry, Sheep/Goat/Piggery, Fisheries, Dairy development, Forestry, Storage & Market yards, IRDP and other non-farm sector. According to 1995-96 about 1149 such schemes were sanctioned with the total disbursement of Rs 3922 crores.

(5) Science & Technology

The application of Science and Technology to agriculture, industry, transports and for all other economic and non-economic activities has become essential for rapid economic development. The council of Scientific and Industrial Research (CSIR), The Indian Council of Agriculture Research (ICAR) are helping the economic sectors for adoption of improved technologies for the production. In the mean time, Technology missions have been introduced to bring about significant improvements in the fields of drinking water, immunisation, oilseeds, literacy, telecommunications, and dairy. The core inputs of the technology mission are people's participation and application of Science and Technology for the development in the areas referred to above. The said missions engaged in the rectification of old technologies and adoption of new one in more scientific manner. Some of the missions able to attain tremendous success.

(6) Social Overheads

The Social overheads comprises of health, hygiene and education etc.

The constitution of India lays down that "the state shall regard the raising of level of nutrition and the standard of living of its people and the improvement of public health as among its primary duties." To give effect to this directive, health has been given due priority. Public Health is primarily the responsibility of the State Governments. The Central Government, however, guides, sponsors and supports major schemes for improving the health of the people. The Ministry of Health and Family Welfare Co-ordinates the work of the State Governments. The Central Council of Health advises the ministry on policies and programmes in all their aspects. The latest information indicates that nearly 56 per cent of hospitals accounting for 30 per cent of beds were under the ownership of private or voluntary organisations while 44 per cent of hospitals with about 70 per cent beds were under government run facilities and were looked after by the local bodies. Thus, the hospitals run by government were fewer in number and much-too overcrowded in terms of beds. It is evident that, only one-third of the number of hospitals with only 20 per cent of the number of beds in the country are located in rural areas. These lower proportions of government managed public health facilities and locations in rural areas speaks about the scarce attention given to the provision of public health facilities for the masses, resulting in its lop-sided availability for the poor as against the urban affluent classes of population in the country. In the opinion of those concerned among the medical profession, what needs urgent attention is expansion of facilities providing simple and cheap but effective preventive health care rather than the prevalent emphasis on sophisticated, personalised, expensive and urban-based medical services.

Human Resource Development is an integral part of the programmes aiming at improving the quality of life, and extension of educational facilities is an essential effort in that direction. The working group on education has recognised education as a crucial input in the process of human resource development. Economic and social development plans of the country have invariably stressed that for the improvement of the quality of life of every individual there has to be an investment in man. The government is therefore, keen that education should find its right place in national planning and the investments in education should find its right place in national planning and the investments in education should reflect its pivotal role. The realisation of this basic purpose, education systems and programmes are expected to be redirected towards a set of goals and tasks among which, the most important are. (i) To guarantee equality of opportunity for all in education to improve their quality of life and to participate in the tasks of promoting the general well being of the society. (ii) To afford all young people and adults irrespective of age, the means for self-fulfillment within the frame-work of a harmonious development which reflects the needs of the community (iii) To provide for a continuous process of life long education for their physical, intellectual and cultural development and for inculcating capabilities to cope with and influence social changes (iv) to establish dynamic and beneficial links between education, employment and development with due regard for the economic and social aims of community and (v) to promote the values of national integration, secularism, democratic way of life and dignity of labour. It is evident that, Education is a key input in breaking the vicious circle of poverty and low productivity. The literacy rate in the country according to 1991 Census was just above half of the population i.e; 52.1 per cent while the male literacy was 64.1 per cent and the female literacy was 39.3 per cent. The rate of literacy in rural and urban areas was 45 per cent and 73 per cent respectively in the same period. A number of steps were taken to increase the level of literacy but the goal is not achieved till date. Greater attention needs to be paid to this sector.

Per Capita Income

India is rich in natural resources and manpower. These resources however not been exploited fully and are capable of greater utilisation. The Per capita Gross National Product for India was estimated at US $ 380. This is about 71 times less than the per capita GNP of industrialised countries and 13 times less than the world average. However, the per capita Net National Products/Income stood at Rs 9578 in the year 1995-96. It is also evident that the NNP is ill distributed among the states of the country. The slow growth rate of GNP and NNP and faster rate of growth of population results India as a poor country. The situation in rural areas is worse in our country. The contribution of rural sector is about one-third of the gross domestic product. The growth rates during Eighth Plan shows that the Economy achieved a total growth rate of about 6.8 per cent. The sectoral growth rate shows that, agriculture and allied activities was 4 per cent, mining & quarrying 3.5 per cent, manufacturing 9.2 per cent, electricity & water supply 7.4 per cent, construction 5.2 per cent, transport 9 per cent, communication 14.9 per cent and other services 5.6 per cent. The percentage share of agriculture & allied sector to GDP was 27 per cent on 1996-97.

The State

Orissa is one of the Twenty- fifth states of India. Its geographical location is given by its extension from 810 - 27'E to 870-29'E Longitudes and 170-49'N to 220-34'N Latitudes on the eastern coast of India. It covers an area of about 155,707 square kilometres. It is a maritime state with a coastal line of about 266 Miles along with the Bay of Bengal. It is bounded by Bay of Bengal in the east. Madhya Pradesh in West, Bihar in the North, West Bengal in North-east and Andhra Pradesh in the South.

Geographical Feature

The State has two major physiographic divisions, i.e; the coastal plains and the high lands and plateaus of Orissa.

The State's major rivers flowing towards the Bay of Bengal have formed the coastal plains. This region is the most developed part of the state due to its fertile and productive alluvial soil.

The highlands and plateaus of the state are having four conspicuous sub-regions. The sub-regions are the Eastern Ghats, which are abruptly and steeply in the east and slope gently to a dissected plateau in the west running north-east (Mayurbhanj district) to south west (Koraput district). The next region is the subdued plateaus, which are the part of Eastern Ghats. This tract separates the eastern coastal plains from the rolling uplands of Western Orissa. The rolling uplands that are another region of the division are lower in elevation. These are situated as discontinuous tracts both in the northern and southern parts and are divided into a number of uplands forming lower order physiographic units due to continued action of rivers running over them.

Climate

The climate of the state is more or less of extreme type. The month of May is the hottest month, where the maximum temperature is varying from 33.3^{0}C to 47.3^{0}C. The December month is the coldest month in the state, where the minimum temperature is varying from 11.6^0 C to 13.9^{0}C. The Sundergarh district experiences both the hottest and coldest temperature in the state. The mean relative humidity varies from the maximum of 82 per cent to minimum of 51 per cent. The average annual normal rainfall in the state is 1482 mm. This rainfall is received through the South-West monsoon from June to September.

Administrative Setup

The state is divided into 30 districts from the administrative point of view. There are, 58 Sub-divisions, 147 Tahasils, 314 Community Development Blocks, 5263 Grampanchayats having 46,989 Inhabited and 4068 Unihabited villages. There are also, 124 towns, 424 police stations.

Demography

The total population of the state was 316 lakhs according to 1991 Census. Among them 160 lakhs are male and 156 lakhs are female population. They comprise 50.6 per cent and 49.4 per cent as male and female population respectively. Besides, 274 lakhs i.e; 86.7 per cent of the total population live in the rural areas whereas the rest 42 lakhs i.e; 13.3 per cent live in urban areas of the state. The total Scheduled Caste and Scheduled Tribe population was 51 lakhs and 70 lakhs respectively. This comprises of about 16.1 per cent and 22.2 per cent respectively of the total population. The density of population is 203 persons per square kilometer. This is distributed as 179 persons and 1665 persons per square kilometer in rural and urban areas of the State respectively. The sex ratio in the state shows continuous decline in females to male population, which was 971 females per 1000 males in the state. The same was 981:1000 in 1981 census. The rate of literacy in the State was 49.1 per cent as against 52.1 per cent in all India.

Workforce

The total workforce of the state was 119 lakhs according to 1991 census. Among them 104 lakhs treated as main workers and 15 lakhs as Marginal workers. They constitute about 87.4 per cent and 12.6 per cent respectively to the total workers in the state. It is also observed that, there are 46 lakh cultivators, 30 lakh agricultural labourers, 3 lakh engaged in household industries and rest 25 lakh employed in other economic activities. They are 44.2 per cent, 28.8 per cent, 2.9 per cent and 24.1 per cent respectively to the total main workers in the state.

Rural and Urban Distribution of Workforce

The participation rate of workers* in the State for urban and rural areas was 29.7 per cent and 38.7 per cent respectively. The alternative source of livelihood is limited in the rural areas. Due to this, the pressure of population is considerably high on land. Nearly 63.8 per cent of the total working population is engaged directly or indirectly in agricultural sector. The share of workers belonging to household industries and other than household industry sector stood at 23.6 per cent according to 1991 census. In the rural areas, the participation rate of women was 22.6 per cent, whereas, the same was only 8.1 per cent in the urban areas according to 1991 census.

---

*The Census of India defined "worker", "non-worker" and "marginal worker" in the following lines; "Those who had worked for the major part of the year. By major part of the year is meant six months (183 days) or more are termed as "main workers". Those who have not worked for the major part of the year i.e; for less than six months (183 days) in the year termed as "marginal workers". A person irrespective of age and whether educated or not, if he or she reports that he or she is not engaged in any other activity called "Non-workers

Unemployment

It has estimated that the total backlog of unemployment at the end of Seventh Plan was 7.30 lakh. The annual addition of labour force being 2.70 lakh, the total addition of labour force during two annual plans, i.e; 1990-91 and 1991-92 would be 5.40 lakhs and the estimated generation of employment was of the order of 5.68 lakh. Hence, at the beginning of Eighth Plan the total backlog of unemployment was 7.02 lakh. Taking this into consideration. It was estimated that the total backlog of unemployment would be at 10.20 lakh in the year 1997-98.

Poverty

The incidence of poverty in Orissa is the highest among major states of the country. According to the Report of the Expert Group of Planning Commission, about 48.6 per cent of the State's population live below the poverty line. The rural poverty stood at 49.7 per cent and it is the highest among all the states as well as the national average of 37.3 per cent, according to 1993-94 estimation. The incidence of rural poverty was about 67.3 per cent in 1973-74. It shows that, the incidence of rural poverty has declined to about 17.6 per cent over a period of twenty years. This clearly indicates that the rate of decline is less than one per cent per annum. If the rate of decline will continue at this rate then it will require another 50 years to alleviate the poverty in rural Orissa.

Agriculture

Agriculture is the main stay of the State's economy and sustenance of the life of the people. It provides employment opportunities to about 65 per cent of the total population and contributes nearly 36 per cent to the net State Domestic Product. The contribution of agricultural sector to the industry and Trade and Commerce sector is also more. In the State like ours, most of the people engaged themselves in agro-based industries. Likewise, agricultural products are the main source of trade and commerce.

Land Resources

Land is the basic and most important input of agriculture. This is declining gradually over the years due to its use for purposes other than agriculture. There are about 6 lakh small and marginal farmers and 30 lakh agricultural labourers in the State. Most of them are landless and assetless. The lands of the state are mostly sub-divided, fragmented and scattered for which the holdings are utterly deficient and uneconomic. In the state the marginal and un-economic holdings account for about 78 per cent of the total holdings. This causes low agricultural productivity in the state. The occurrence of natural calamities at regular interval also has adverse effect on agriculture.

In Orissa about 21.63 lakh hectares of cultivated land are irrigated of the total, 9.72 lakh hectares were irrigated through major and medium irrigation projects, 3.96 lakh hectare and 2.87 lakh hectare of land were irrigated through minor flow and minor Lift irrigation projects respectively. The remaining 5.08 lakh hectares of cultivated land were irrigated through other sources. The percentage of net area irrigated in relation to the cultivable area was 37.4 per cent. This is much less than that of developed states of the country.

Fertilizers

The per hectare consumption of chemical fertilizer in Orissa is also very less compared to National average. The per hectare consumption of chemical fertilizer in Orissa was only 24.6 kg in 1996-97, whereas this stood at 75.7 kgs at national level.

Foodgrain Production

In the Foodgrain Production, the percentage share of Orissa to the national total was only about 4.0 per cent. The State's percapita foodgrain production was 18.2 kg as against rational average of about 20.6 kg. This position has remained almost static over years. The cultivation and production of paddy continued to be higher, this is, more than 90 per cent of the total.

Live Stock

According to the live stock census of 1991 the total live stock population of Orissa was stood at 230 lakh. There are 135.8 lakh catttles including 5.6 lakh-crossbred cattle. There are also 18.4 lakh sheeps, 48.0 lakh goats and 5.9 lakh pigs. The percapita daily availability of milk was only about 46 grams as against 183 grams at all India level.

Fishery

The inland Fishery in the state includes Fresh water and brackish water resources in the area of 6.5 lakh hectares and 5.2 lakh hectares respectively. The total production of fish in the state was 258.0 thousand Million Tonnes. Of the total about 47.3 per cent of fish produced by Fresh water, 5.0 per cent in Brackish water and the remaining 47.7 per cent in Marine waters.

Forest

The total area of about 56060 Sq. Kms is covered by forest. This accounted for about 33.4 per cent of the total geographical area of the state.

Power

Orissa continues to be a power deficit state despite of considerable importance laid for the generation of electricity by Government. However, the rural electrification programme has been successfully implemented in the State. In Orissa about 70 per cent of villages have been electrified. Among them 54 per cent of Tribal villages and 93 per cent of Scheduled Caste villages have been electrified.

Mineral Resources

Orissa has vast mineral resources and other raw materials.

The State occupies an important position both in terms of mineral deposits and its production. It shares 18.4 per cent of the total mineral deposits and contributes to 8.7 per cent of the total production in the country. Orissa is rich in bauxite, chromite, coal, graphite, dolomite, iron ore, manganese, nickel and vanadium. The mineral resource of the state has not exploited. This is due to lack of infrastructural facilities, low rate of investment and labour problems. According to 1991 census about 1 lakh persons engaged in mining and quarrying activities in the state. It can be stated here that, the proper exploitation of mineral resources and the development of industries based on them would help to bring about a total change of industrial map of the State.

Industry

Orissa has a long and illustrious tradition of producing through its artisans exquisitely beautiful arts and crafts, which would be the feast of mankind. The state is endowed with vast mineral resources including precious stones, fertile land, perennial rivers, large tracts of forest, abundant flora and fauna and long coastline. Despite continued planning process, the state still remain deficient in physical infrastructure, industrial investment, entrepreneurial ability, skilled manpower and exploitation of natural resources.

The percapita investment in industries in Orissa was (1961) much lower than all major states and National average (Rs 2303). The number of registered working factories per lakh of population in the state was only 4.6. This is much lower compared to the major states and the all-India average, where this was stood at 13.0.

In Orissa, there are 276 large and medium scale industries with total investment of Rs 1168 crores and employment potential of about 75 thousand persons.

There are about 48 thousand small-scale industries in the State with total investment of about Rs 804 crores creating employment opportunities for about 3.5 lakh persons.

In the state there are, 12,56 lakh artisan units in the state with an investment of about Rs 31592 crores. The total employment opportunity of the sector is 21.56 lakh persons. Khadi and village industries also plays important role in rural industrialisation of the state. The Government undertakings and potential agencies like IDC, IPICOL, OSFC, OSIC, OFDC and DICs have been maintaining their efforts to assist in the growth of industrial units in the State.

Orissa has vast potentials for development of tourism, which have remained largely untapped. With a view to promoting development of tourism industries a number of tourism related activities have been treated as industrial activities. Orissa Tourism Development Corporation (OTDC) is looking for the development of such activities.

The rural trade activity refers to the retail trade and small business. The said activity is providing livelihood to a substantial group of rural population in the State. It is evident that the rural trade activities are mostly dominated by the agricultural products, forest products and products of village and cottage industries. These products generally are produced and sold in local markets. However, due to low productivity low investment, the trade activity in the rural areas has not been developed. Besides, the inadequate infrastructural facilities act as a major obstacle for the promotion of the trade and business in rural areas of the state.

INFRASTRUCTURE

In Orissa, the total road length of Orissa was 218.4 thousand kilometers. The total road length of National Highway was 1.6 thousand kilometers; State Highway was 4.4 thousand kilometers. The total District road length of the State was 9.5 thousand kilometers. There are 10.0 thousand kilometers belong to Municipalities of the State, where as the total rural road length of the state was 192.9 thousand kilometers. This includes forest and irrigation roads. The length of surface road per 100 square kilometer of area was 12.4 kilometers as against 29.3 kilometers at all-India level. The average road length per lakh of population was 568 kilometers in the state as against 246 kilometers at the all-India level.

In Orissa, the total railway route length in the State was about 2178 kilometers comprising of 2035 kilometers of Broad gauge and 143 kilometers of Narrow gauge. The railway route length per thousand square kilometers was 14.0 kilometers in the state as against 19.0 kilometers at the all-India level.

In respect of water transport, rivers and sea are notable. Paradeep and Gopalpur are the major port of the State; this plays a strategic and pivotal role in area of Cargo handling. There are also inland water transport facilities in the State.

The state capital is also connected in air with major cities of the country. The capital is well connected with the cities like, Delhi, Mumbai, Chennai, Calcutta, Hyderabad and Visakhapatnam in air.

Post Office & Telegraphs

In the state, there are more than 8 thousand Post-offices and 24 Telegraph offices. The population per post-office in Orissa was about 4.0 thousand as against 5.8 thousand at all-India level. The average area under one post-office was 19.3 square kilometre in Orissa as against 21.5 square kilometer in the country.

Education

The teacher pupil ratio in Orissa was 36,32,22 in primary, middle and secondary and higher secondary institutions respectively. This was 64,37 and 17 at the all-India level. The percapita expenditure on Education was Rs 245 in the state as against Rs 313 at the all-India level.

Health Services

In Orissa, there are 185 PHCs, 700 additional PHCs, 180 Hospitals, 157 CHCs and 150 Dispensaries to cater to the needs of the people. Besides, there are 42 Medical aid centres, 171 HSCs, 32 MHCs, 5 Ayurvedic Hospitals, 537 Ayurvedic Dispensaries, 4 Homeopathic Hospitals and 478 Homeopathic Dispensaries in the State. The number of persons per hospital bed in Orissa was about 2.2 thousand persons as against 1.5 thousand persons at all-India level. Likewise, one registered Medical Practitioner have to serve about 2.8 thousand persons in Orissa as against 2.1 thousand at all-India. At present the State has 3 Medical Colleges, 1 Nurshing College, 1 Dental College and 1Pharmacy College. Besides, there are 6 Homeopathic Colleges ad 5 Ayurvedic Colleges in the State, to facilitate health education, training and services.

Financial Institutions

The Financial institutions of the State comprises of Co-operatives, Commercial Banks, Regional Rural Banks. Above all there are RBI and NABARD.

Cooperatives

The cooperatives may be classified into two such as; credit cooperatives, and non-credit cooperatives. The credit cooperatives in the State are of two types, short and medium term cooperatives, and long-term cooperatives. The short and medium terms cooperative are in three-tier system in the apex there is State Cooperative Bank. In the middle there are 17 Central Cooperative Banks and at the base level 5878 Cooperative Societies are functioning. The long-term cooperatives are two tier systems. There is Orissa State Cooperative Agricultural and Rural Development Bank at the State level. At the grass root level there are 57 Cooperative Agricultural and Rural Development Bank.

The State Cooperative Bank is the scheduled Bank. Total membership of the bank was 4131 with working capital of Rs 578 crores. The deposit and loans advanced of the Bank was Rs 239 crores and Rs318 crores in 1996-97.

The total membership of Central Cooperative Banks in the

State was 22.9 thousand with working capital of Rs909 crores. The total deposit of the Banks was Rs496 crores and advance was Rs292 crores, according to the year 1996-97.

In the State, there are about 2808 Primary Agricultural Credit Societies with the membership of about 35 thousand in 1996-97. The total deposits mobilised by the societies were Rs 85.4 crores and loans advanced was Rs181.4 crores in the year under observation.

There is a Orissa State Cooperative Agricultural Rural Development Bank (OSCARD). The Cooperative Agricultural Rural Development Banks (CARD) is the member of the former bank. The working capital of the OSCARD Bank was Rs 145 crores in the year 1996-97. The deposits and advance of the bank was Rs 1.2 crore and Rs 14.25 crore respectively. The total working capital of the CARD banks in the state was Rs 147 cores. Where as, the deposit and advance of the bank was Rs 4.6 crores and Rs 12.5 cores in the year 1996-97.

The average membership per society is reported to be stood at 906. In the State about 83 per cent of total population covered by co-operatives, where as this is only 64 per cent for rural areas on 1996-97.

Commercial Banks

In the State, there are 2170 Branches of scheduled commercial banks. Of the total the share of offices functioning in rural areas was 76.4 per cent. The total deposits mobilised by the bank was Rs 8817.5 crores in 1996. The contribution of rural areas was 30.4 per cent. The loan advanced by scheduled commercial banks was Rs 3291.8 crores in the said year. The share of rural areas was 36.5 per cent. The population coverage per branch in Orissa was 15 thousand as against 14 thousand per branch at all-India level.

Regional Rural Banks (RRBs)

There are 822 branches of 9 Regional Rural Banks in the state. The total deposits mobilised by the RRBs was Rs 350.5

crores in the year 1997-98 where as the total loans advanced by the banks was Rs 260.4 crores.

Other Financial Institutions

In Orissa, there are industrial and financial institutions like, IDBI, ICICI, IFCI and Investment institutions like, LIC, GIC, UTI and OSFC, IPICOL are the state level institutions.

NABARD

National Bank for Agriculture and Rural Development (NABARD) is the apex bank for Agricultural Credit and Rural development. It provides credit to the farmers and people belong to other rural economic activities through commercial Banks, Regional Rural Banks and Cooperative Banks. The total refinance assistance of NABARD for various purposes in Orissa in the year 1997-98 was stood at Rs.128.3 crores. At the same time NABARD provided refinance assistance to about 16 schemes under agriculture and Rural development. The important Schemes/programmes that, received refinance assistance are (1) Minor irrigation (2) Land development (3) Farm mechanism (4) Plantation & Horticulture (5) Fishery (6) Forestry and waste land development (7) Dairy development (8) Bio-gas (9) Poultry (10) IRDP/SGSY (11) SC/ST - AP/ITDP (12) PMRY (13) Self-Help Groups (14) Non-farm sector (15) Sheep/goat/piggery (16) Other farm sectors.

Pre-dominance of the Rural Sector

- In India, about Three-Fourth of its population live in rural areas.
- The distribution of work force in the country indicates that about 79.2 per cent of the total workers depend on rural economic activities for their livelihood.
- The concentration of un-employment and under employment is high in rural areas. The traditional economic sectors in the rural areas failed to provide ad-equate and appropriate employment

opportunities to the increasing rural masses. This is perhaps due to rapid growth of population and changing attitude of employment.

- The poverty in rural areas is deep seated with 49.7 per cent of the total population live below poverty line in Orissa and 37.3 per cent at all-India level. This is the major constraint for development.

- Agricultural sector provide livelihood to about two-third of the total population and three-fourth of the rural population. Most of the small and marginal farmers live in rural areas of the country. The Agricultural labourers and non-agricultural labourers are also belonging to the countryside. The productivity of the sector and the living standard of the people attached to the sector is remaining under developed. Special attenention is needed for the development of the important economic sector.

- Allied activities to agriculture comprises of animal husbandry, poultry, fishery and forestry etc. These activities play very important role in rural economy. It is also evident that, the economic weaker sections, particularly, small and marginal farmers, agricultural and non-agricultural labourers are availing alternative employment opportunities during lean agriculture seasons. Besides, a considerable percentage or rural people depend on this sector for their livelihood. Despite of its importance in the economy the sector is remain underdeveloped. This sector requires more attention for its development.

- The Small - Scale Industries, village, cottage and other artisan based industries play a prominent role in the rural economy. Despite of its importance, the sector and the artisans in particular remain neglected. This is perhaps due to application of traditional and years old Techniques of Production, lack of awareness, education and above all inadequate attention in economic planning, implementation etc. As an important economic sector, it requires more attention.

- The rural areas of the country is also lacking adequate infrastructure. The promotion of the infrastructural facilities is the essential condition for the attainment of economic development as well as rural development in the country.
- Institutional credit regarded as one of the important input for transformation of the rural economic activities from traditional to modern. It is observed that the rural area of the country is inadequately served with the credit institutions.
- The social overheads comprises of Health, Nutrition, Education etc. are also not developed up to the required level after 50 years of planned economic development in the country. The situation in rural areas is reported to be precarious.

As against this background, the Socio-economic upliftment in the rural areas needs greater attention.

The planners, policy makers have given utmost attention for the attainment of Economic development through rural development. Greater emphasis has been given for the rural development during different plan periods. Beginning from the First Five Year Plan (1950-51) priority has been given for the rural development. A number of rural development programmes/schemes has also been initiated in this respect. Despite of Multi-dimensional plans for rural development the desired goal has not been achieved till date. As against this background, a humble attempt is made to highlight important rural development programmes/schemes, initiated/ introduced/ implemented in our country, since First Plan period to the end of Eighth Plan Period (1992-97). A little attempt was also made to highlights the plan approaches and strategies for rural development in India.

2

PLAN APPROACH FOR RURAL DEVELOPMENT

The definition of Rural is residuary become all over the world that is defined as an urban area and whatever is not urban known as rural. In India a settlement is defined as urban if it fulfils either of the following conditions, were adopted in the 1991 census;

(i) All statutory towns, i.e; all places with a municipality corporation, municipality board, cantonment board or notified town area etc.

(ii) A minimum population of 5,000.

(iii) At least 75 per cent of the Male working population engaged in non-agricultural and allied activity.

(iv) A density of population of at least 400 persons per square kilometres.

Thus, the term 'Rural' essentially means an area, which is characterised as non-urban style of life, occupational structure and settlement pattern.

'Development' in general refers to the process of a general improvement in levels of living together, decreasing inequality in incomes and the capacity to sustain continuous improvements overtime.

Thus the term Rural Development is viewed as an activity of a series of activities or a process, which either improves the immediate living conditions-economic, social, political, cultural and environmental or increases the potential for future living or both of the rural people.

The Royal commission on Agriculture defined Rural Development as,

"We can not too strongly state our conviction that the directorship of agriculture is one of the key posts in Rural Development and that agricultural advance must in a very great degree depend upon the stability of the officer."

The taskforce appointed by the Planning Commission on Integrated Rural Development in 1972 defined Rural Development as;

"After a careful consideration we have belatedly decided to take what might be considered a rather restricted view of the expression. 'Rural Development' we have chose to equate it with agricultural development in the widest sense so as to embrace besides crop husbandry, all the allied activities."

According to the view of World Bank "Rural Development as a strategy design to improve the economic and social life of a specific group of people - The rural (people) poor. It involves extending the benefits of development to the poorer among those who seek a livelihood in rural areas. The group includes small-scale farmers, tenants and the landless."

Rural Development means a strategy to improve the economic and social life of the rural poor and the rural weak in the overall spectrum of development and growth. It is not only important to raise the agricultural productivity and the rate of overall economic growth in the rural areas, but also it is to ensure that the poor and weaker sections share the benefit.

"Rural Development as a process in complex and involves the interaction of economic, social, political, technological and other situational factors. These have to be integrated with Government policies and plans with the objective of improving the quality of life of the people in the villages".

Rural Development encompasses (i) Improvement in levels

of living, including employment, education, health and nutrition housing and a variety of social services (ii) decreasing inequality in distribution of rural incomes and in rural-urban balances in incomes and economic opportunities and (iii) The capacity of the rural sector to sustain and accelerate the pace of these improvements.

The critical element in the Rural Development is improvement living standards of the poor through opportunities for better utilisation of their physical and human resources in the absence of this utilisation of rural resources has no functional significance. Making the process of rural development self-sustaining of capital and use of technology for the benefit of the poor but their active involvement in the building up of institutions as well as functioning of these.

There are a number of definitions of rural development. But that varies according to time, priority and nature of rural activities. Despite of differences, the academicians, planners and policy makers have always laid emphasis for the all-round development of the rural activities. However, Rural Development as a concept and as series of experiments in alternative methods of organising production, welfare and exchange in rural activities has a long history and is not the monopoly of any single system or country. Its recent popularity however is mainly symptomatic of the failure of technocratic and growth strategies pursued by most developing countries in the 1950s and 1960s. Academics, nationals and international policy makers are carrying out the search for solution to the twin problems of rural poverty and unemployment. The noted Western economists like, Kuznets, Gerschenkron, Floud and Mccloskey provide useful insights into the history of economic development of the present day developed countries. The growth of output and productivity in these countries during last 10 to 15 decades has been qualitatively different from that observed in earlier periods. Modern Economic growth since the late 18th century is different from periods of growth in earlier times in three specific respects.

Firstly, the ownership and use of economic surplus were

separated for the first time. Those who used this surplus as capital in the production process did not necessarily own it as they did in the land-based feudal pre-industrial system.

Secondly, extensive use of an acceptable unit of exchange called money helped in expansion of market, which made specialization and mobility possible.

Lastly, mobility of both capital and labour in pursuit of higher gains to urban areas and distant lands occurred on an unprecedented scale. The consequent increase in output and productivity were substantial and sustained over a long period of time. These impressive increases were also accompanied by growth of population and large-scale migration from not only rural to urban areas but from nation to nation and from continent to continent.

Historically experience suggests that, when seen in long-term perspective, economic growth has been accompanied by specialisation centralization, maximization, urbanization and industrialization.

History shows that, poverty has been diminished by the growth of labour increased productivity in the agricultural sector and migration of labour to urban non-agricultural activities. The population movement occurred mainly because industry could offer the incentive of higher wages and better employment opportunities.

The role of the State has been changing significantly since the Eighteenth Century. Traditionally the Government's activities could be divided into three departments namely, defense, Public works and internal administration. A healthy balance among the three ensured stable regimes with the advent of modern economic development; the "Public works" component has been an expanding area of State activity.

Modern development policy makers while, recognising the importance of infrastructure have been rather ambiguous about the contents of infrastructure is one of the very few illuminating contributions on the subject. Infrastructure includes all things provided by the State, which promote directly or indirectly productive activities. Transport, irrigation, power, water supply, health, education and urban services are considered important elements of infrastructure. In a mixed economy, with a relatively important public sector, provision of infrastructure has to be carefully planned and provided by the State.

The State playing an important role in development. Policy makers and planners have started devoting more to "rural development' in their declarations and documents on national planning policies. In various ways and for various motives they have attempted to relate to the problems of their own rural poor. Despite, substantial and impressive increase in growth of agricultural and food outputs in some regions of a number of developing countries the plight of small and marginal farmers, agricultural and landless labourers, artisans and small retailers has not been improved significantly.

In India the term 'Rural Development' is not a very old phenomenon. Early in the century their exist the British rule. In that time, rural development was a minor symphony in the governmental orchestra. The functions of the Government were limited and even the spread of each function was narrowly restricted. Thus, Development cannot but be of minor meaning and significance in the structure of the priorities of colonialism, which was also reflected in the rural areas.

The decade 1920-30 was very significant from the view of early pioneering efforts at rural development in India. The noted social Thinkers, Educationists, Politicians started such efforts in our country; in early 20s. The important activities and experiments undertaken for rural development in Pre-Independence periods are;

(i) **Sriniketan Experiments:** This programme was pioneered by noted scholar of the country Rabindranath Tagore. The important objective of the experiment was Economic and Moral rehabilitation of the rural community.

(ii) **Martandum Project:** One Rural Reconstruction Programme was initiated by Spancer Hatch at

Martandum (South Travancore) in 1921. Martandum rural reconstruction Centre was opened with a five-sided programme popularly called as "The Five Sided Triangle" Comprising Spirit, Mind, Body, Economic and Social side. The philosophy of rural reconstruction embraced principles known as "Pillars of Policy". The principle of 'Self Help' was maintained. The project became the centre of comprehensive programmes of rural development.

(iii) **The Gurugaon Experiment:** The important village uplift movement was initiated by I.L.Brayne the Deputy Commissioner of Gurugaon district in 1920. This village development programme called as the "Gurugaon Scheme". The Gurugaon Scheme claimed to deal with the whole life and the activity of the peasant and his family and to present a complete remedy from the terrible conditions in with they lived.

(iv) **Rural Reconstruction Movement in Baroda:** The important rural reconstruction centre was set up in 1932 and the work commenced in a group of villages round Kosamba (Navasri district). The movement aimed at improvement in all aspect of rural life, changing the outlook of the agriculturists, the attainment of higher standard of living.

(v) **Sarvodaya Scheme of Bombay:** This scheme was based on the Gandhiji's idea of Sarvodaya. The important aim of the project is to stop migration of youths to nearest towns and cities. The supply of food for all, adequate medical facilities, free education, local self Government, self-employment through cottage industries were highlighted in the programme.

(vi) **Firka Development Scheme:** The Firka Development Scheme aimed at the attainment of the Gandhian ideal of "Village Swaraj" by brining about not only the education, economic, sanitary and other improvements of village along with the revitalisation of the spirit if people and to make them self-confident and self-reliant. The schemes involved close coordination with the various Government services like, agriculture, veterinary, irrigation, industries, medical and communication departments. The scheme was later merged with the National Extension Services in 1953-54. Programmes and projects were also launched in post independence and pre-planning periods. The important among them are;

(1) The Pilot Development Project of Etawah

The Project began under the sponsorships of the provincial Governments of Uttarpradesh in late 1948.

The important objectives of the project were to increase the degree of productivity, social improvements, promotion of self-confidence and cooperation.

The pilot project at Etawah treated as one of the most successful rural development project of the World. The project also exhibited the exemplary Cooperation and Coordination of Government, volunteers and others.

(2) The Nilokheri Experiment

India divided in 1947. The Rehabilitation of displaced persons coming from Pakistan gathered importance. In order to provide them gainful employment a new township was developed at Nilokheri in 1948 with the efforts of Sri S.K.Dey. Sri Dey evolved a faith were to activate and support a triple charter of rights such as; (i) Right to live, (ii) Right to work for living and (iii) right to receive what is earned. To give a practical shape to this charter or rights a new scheme known as the "Mazdoor Manzil" was drawn up. The basic concept of the Mazdoor Manzil was to stop the one-way traffic of labour, material, skill and culture from villages to town. The township was intended to include institutions for medical relief and sanitation, Higher Education, Technical and Vocational Training, Veterinary aid and agricultural extension embracing agriculture, horticulture, poultry, piggery, fishery, sheep breeding and other forms of animal husbandry. The project was highly appreciated by the then Prime Minister Pandit Jawaharlal Nehru.

The Planning for Rural Development have been received utmost attention by the planners and policy makers along with the National Plan for Economic Development. The rural development strategies were also adopted by planners as per the methods and strategies adopted for the economic development of the country. India adopted both the centralised and decentralised planning models in the process of its planned economic development.

The First Five Year Plan (1950-51 to 1955-56) adopted the Harrod-Domar model of capital accumulation and saving mobilisation as its methodological approach towards planning. Under this approach, the process of economic development must start from the villages. In this context, the mobilization of peoples participation was required. In order to implement this ideology the Community Development Programme (CDP) was conceived. The Block administration was created as a centre of Rural Development activities. This programme failed as blocks were quite big and left the weaker section untouched. The programme was also implemented in Orissa. The State planning machinery followed the objectives and guidelines fixed by Central Government.

The Second Five Year Plan (1955-56 to 1960-61) based on Feldman-Mahalnobis model of sectoral growth. This strategy emphasised investment in heavy industry to achieve industrialization, which was assumed to be the basic condition for rapid economic development. A good deal of reliance was placed on cottage and small industries with the aim of reducing rural under employment, unemployment. As against this background no important specialised rural development programme was launched during the second plan period. However, steps were taken to strengthen the ongoing community development programme. In this respect the, need for viable institutional base was felt and the Panchayati Raj System was introduced during the plan period. Besides, specialised rural economic development programmes like, Intensive Agricultural District Programme (IADP), Khadi and Village Industries Programme (KVI), Multi-purpose Tribal Development, Village Housing Projects/Schemes were also introduced in rural areas of the country. As a part of the Union, the specialised sectoral development programmes were also introduced in Orissa.

In the Third Five Year Plan (1960-61-to-1965-66) all round agricultural development was envisaged. Increased agricultural production in the farm sector and activities allied to agriculture received topmost priority during the plan period. The important agricultural development programmes bringing green revolution strategy like Intensive Agricultural Area Programme (IAAP) and High Yield Varieties Programme (HYVP) were implemented in the country. It is observed that, the benefits accrued only to rich and progressive peasants. Once again, landless and agricultural labourers were left untouched. Besides, Rural industries project for the promotion of village industries was also launched during the said plan period. Health and Nutrition is regarded as important inputs required for improvement in the quality of life. To ensure appropriate and adequate nutrition to the children, for their growth Applied Nutrition Programme was introduced during the Third Five Year Plan.

The Fourth Five Year Plan (1969-74) in the name of "Growth with social justice" initiated efforts towards uplifting the vulnerable sections of rural society. In this connection a number of 'area development oriented' and 'Target Oriented' programmes were introduced. Programmes such as Small Farmers Development Agency (SFDA), Small Farmers and Agricultural Labourers Development Agency (MFAL), Drought Prone Area Programme (DPAP), Tribal Area Development Programme (TADP) were introduced as the important rural development programmes. These rural development programmes did succeed, but only in limited areas and numbers. This plan paved the path for a number of rural development and poverty alleviation programmes in the country. These programmes were implemented through the existing administrative apparatus at block and village levels. Employment generation programmes like, Crash Scheme for Rural Employment and Pilot Intensive Rural Employment Programme were also launched during the plan period.

The Fifth Plan (1974-79) based on the Inter-sectoral transactions model of leontif which emphasised on strengthening the intersectoral linkages for balanced growth in sectors. The most important objectives of the Fifth Plan Period was; (i) removal of poverty and (ii) achievement of self-reliance. In order to attain these objectives, The Programmes like, Command Area Development Programme (CADP), Hill Area Development Programme (HADP), Minimum Needs Programme (MNP), Food For Work Programme (FFW) were introduced, during the plan period. Besides, in order to promote small-scale, village and cottage industries the District Industries Centres (DICs) were set up in all districts of the country. The 20-point Economic Programme was also introduced during the said plan period.

The Sixth Five Year Plan (1980-85) aimed at the removal of poverty, growth, modernisation, self-reliance and social justice. In order to attain all-round development in rural areas, one single integrated programme called Integrated Rural Development Programme (IRDP) was conceived. IRDP is regarded as a multi-level, multi-sector and multi-section concept of rural development. As a multi-level concept it encompasses rural development at various levels such as viable cluster of village communities, districts and blocks. As a multi-sector concept, it embraces development in various sectors and sub-sectors of the rural areas such as agriculture, industry, education, health and transportation etc. As a multi-section concept, it encompasses socio-economic development of various sections and sub-sections of rural population such as Small farmers, Marginal farmers, Landless and agricultural labourers, Artisans, Scheduled Castes and Scheduled Tribes. Besides IRDP, the employment generation programmes like, National Rural Employment Programme (NREP), Rural

Landless Employment Guarantee Programme (RLEGP), Economic Rehabilitation or Rural Poor (ERRP), Training of Rural Youth for Self-Employment (TRYSEM), Self Employment for the Educated Unemployed Youths (SEEUY). Development of Women and Children in Rural Areas (DWCRA) etc. were also introduced during the said plan period.

The important objectives of the Seventh Five Year Plan (1985-90) were; building an independent self-reliant economy, establishment of social system based on equity and justice, reduction of regional imbalance and adoption of advanced technologies. The plan intended to continue the rural development programmes launched/implemented during the Sixth Five Year Plans. Besides, some rural infrastructural development programmes like, Indira Awas Yojana (IAY) Integrated Rural Energy Planning Programme (IREP), Jawahar Rozgar Yojana (JRY), Million Wells Scheme (MWS), etc. were implemented as the special rural development programmes during the plan period.

The Eighth Five Year Plan (1992-97) aimed at generation of adequate employment opportunities, Universalisation of elementary education, provision of safe drinking water and primary health care facilities, and strengthening the infrastructure. The special rural development and poverty alleviation programmes implemented in earlier plans were also intended to continue during the Eighth Five Year Plan. In order to boost earlier infrastructure and employment generation programmes the new and culmination programmes like, Intensified Jawahar Rozgar Yojana (IJRY), Employment Assurance Scheme (EAS), Operation Black Board (OBB), and District Primary Education Programme (DPEP) were introduced.

The Ninth Five Year Plan (1997-2002) aimed at generating employment opportunities in the secondary sector, all-round development of agricultural sector, strengthening the rural economy through development of agro-based industries, small-scale village and cottage industries and elimination of poverty. As against these objectives, the programmes for self-employment, and supplementary wage employment and other programmes intended to continue during the Ninth Plan with some modifications. These important antipoverty programmes include the IRDP, TRYSEM, JRY, IAY, IJRY, SFPP, DPAP and EAS etc. The IRDP, DWCRA, TRYSEM, MWS were in operation till the end of 1998-99. It was felt that; this fragmented approach with a multiplicity of schemes was not able to focus on the needs of the rural poor in a coherent manner. Hence these schemes were amalgamated by Government of India and merged into a single new scheme called Swarnajayanti Gram Swarojgar Yojana (SGSY) with effect from 1.4.1999. In order to create adequate infrastructural development the Jawahar Gram Samridhi Yojana (JGSY) was also implemented on the same date.

All the plan strategies for rural development based on various approaches like, growth-based approach in first Three Five Year Plans (First Five Year Plan, Second Five Year Plan, Third Five Year Plan), which was popularly known as trickle down approach. The Fourth Five Year Plan based on Target group approach. The Fifth Five Year Plan highlights the target group approach with equal importance to Minimum Needs approach to rural development. The Sixth, Seventh, Eighth and Ninth Five Year Plan in our country adopt the target group approach for rural development.

The important elements of rural development strategies are,

(1) Appropriate Institutional Arrangements.

(2) Labour - Intensive agriculture and Minor development works.

(3) A hierarchy of development centres to bridge the wide gap between rural and urban areas and self-reliance.

(4) An active policy for social development, and

(5) Appropriate Organisational arrangements.

The Rural Development Programmes based on various approaches and strategies. These are varies according to plan and the Nature of the programme. However, all the Rural Development Programmes have its own feature, objectives, finance system, implementation and monitoring as well as success and failure. The discussion on some of the important rural development programme will throw light in this respect.

3

THE RURAL DEVELOPMENT PROGRAMMES IN INDIA

India started her planned economic development through Five Year Plans in the year 1950-51. The economy of the Country has been dominated by the rural and traditional economic sectors. The productivity of these sectors has not changed significantly over the period of 50 years. The existence of massive unemployment and poverty is the common feature of Indian economy in general and rural economy in particular. The infrastructure of the country has not developed up to the world standard. It is proper to mention here that, we have achieved little over the period of 50 years of planned economic development. The planners and policy makers have been laid best possible efforts for the development of the economy and rural development. Due to a number of factors, desired success has not been achieved so far. However, we would like to discuss some of the important rural development programmes implemented in our country as well as the states and Union Territories from time to time. The aims and objectives of these programmes are national in nature and the progress and achievements are based on the secondary data available. As one of the under developed state, the progress and achievements of rural development programmes of Orissa is also discussed in the chapter. Some comparative analysis of the R.D. Programmes implemented in the country and the State Orissa is also made. Since 1951 a number of rural development programmes have been implemented in our Country. Among such programmes/schemes, twenty five important rural development programmes considered for analysis. These programmes covers all plan periods i.e; First Five Year Plan (1950-51 to 1955-56) to Eighth Five Year Plan (1992-97).

1) Community Development Programme (CDP)

India as an independent Country started its planned economic development process in the year 1950-51. The First Five Year Plan 1950-51 to 1955-56 based on methodical approach. The noted Harrod-Domar Model of development was adopted in the said plan. The model emphasised on capital accumulation and saving. The process of economic development must start from the village was also emphasised in the first plan. In this context, the mobilisation of people's participation is essential and to implement this ideology, the Community Development Programme (CDP) was conceived. The Community Development Programme was launched on 2nd October 1952.

A general village community in India can be divided into six main groups as follows:

(i) The owners of land and those who have hereditary rights of tenancy.

(ii) The sub-tenants or tenants at will.

(iii) Landless Agricultural labourers.

(iv) Village Artisans.

(v) Money lenders and Shopkeepers.

(vi) Persons in the professions or in personal services, e.g. doctors, lawyers, barbers, village officials.

Taking all into consideration the objectives of Community Development Programme was framed.

The important objective of Community Development Programme is to create an urge among the rural people for a better life and to show the way to satisfying this urge predominantly by means of self-help. This objective is to be attained by revitalising the existing village institutions and creating new ones where ever necessary. The programme emphasized to give effects to an intensive and comprehensive programme covering all aspects of rural life; i.e; agriculture, rural industries, education, housing, health, recreation and services etc and aimed at utilising under a democratic set up the surplus labour force in rural areas for development purpose. It also aims at the largest possible extension of the principle of cooperation and every effort to made to make rural families credit worthy.

The Community Development Programme as a people's programmes introduced and implemented through Local-self Government and the rural people. The Local Self Government get further boost after the recommendation of Balwantrai Mehta's formulation of Democratic decentralisation in the forms of village Panchayats, Panchayat Samities and Zilla Parishads.

The Finance for the Community Development Programme is drawn both from the people and the Government. Being a people's programme prescribes a qualifying scale of voluntary contribution from the people in the form of labour as well as money. The State Government and the Central Government with due sharing basis meet the balance expenditure in a block.

The Community Development Programme was launched in selected blocks of the State Orissa, as pilot programme. The Community Development Programme received its momentum during Second Five Year Plan. The total expenditure of Rs 822.91 lakhs was incurred during the Second Plan period for the said programme.

By the end of the Third Five Year Plan (1965-66) period there were 147 Stage I blocks, 139 Stage II blocks bringing the total number of blocks to 314. Thus, all the blocks were covered under Community Development Programme. The total expenditure under this programme was Rs 1767 lakhs.

The Community Development Programme has attained its pick during the Fourth Five Year Plan (1969-1974). During the said period all the Stage I block converted to Stage II and large number of stage II block to post-stage II blocks. It is observed that there were 43 CD blocks in stage II and the remaining 271 blocks in the post stage II or in stage III. Total Fund of Rs 850 lakhs were earmarked for the programme. Besides, special development schemes on irrigation, Agriculture extension, animal husbandry, horticulture, drinking water and communication were also implemented in seven backward districts of the State. In this respect a total sum of Rs 225 lakh has been earmarked.

The contribution of Community Development Programme to the rural development are; (1) The setting up of a network of community development blocks covering the length and breadth of the country, thus enabling the government to reach the rural population in almost any aspect of their life, (2) The transfer of powers and functions for implementing the programme to the elected representatives at the village, block and district levels, thereby paving the way for democratic decentralisation through a three-tier Panchayati Raj System.

The National Institute of Community Development conducted a survey to assess the impact of CDP. They concluded that "the process of modernisation has reached all strata, and going to do so at a faster pace in future, but this has not resulted in any violent reaction on the part of the lower classes".

The ideology of people's participation through Panchayati Raj System, in absence of proper education and discipline resulted in conspicuous alienation of the weaker sections of the rural communities by the privileged classes. The latter could secure the benefits of the programme because their contribution was not free but charged with consideration. It is observed that the whole programme suffered from lack of vitality, and was tending to generate only into a number of material benefits for a limited few.

The official agencies responsibility for implementation of development activities lacked in understanding the new climate because they were manned by those officials who were trained in the particular framework. Besides, their bureaucratic approach also appeared to be a hindrance in initiating the programmes.

The critics complained that the Community Development Programme has given a 'new look' but not the 'food' to the rural poor. It is no denying a fact that the expenditure on building the institutions for social change was larger than the expenditure incurred on productive purposes. Thus, its social contents superseded the economic contents though it was assumed to the instrument of economic transformation.

2) Intensive Agricultural District Programme (IADP)

The Intensive Agricultural District Programme (IADP) as a package programme was very strongly recommended by Agricultural Production Team of the Ford Foundation (USA) on 1959. This programme was put into action during 1960-61.

The important objective of the programme was to improve the agricultural production in a integrated and intensified manner. This programme was introduced in selected districts of the country. The selection of these districts was made on the basis of (a) the district should as far as possible have assured water supply (b) It should have a minimum of natural hazards, (c) It should have well developed village Institutions like Cooperatives and Panchayats (d) It should have maximum potentialities of increasing agricultural production within a comparatively short-time. Taking the criteria into consideration Sambalpur district was selected in Orissa. It was decided to implement for the development of Rabi Crops in 1962-63. This programme was introduced in all the 29 blocks of the district. In the second phase of the programme main thrust was given on the increase of higher yielding paddy in the Khariff extending the area under various commercial and horticulture crops and on promoting efficient soil and water management practices. Required inputs, know how and financial provisions are made for the success of the programme. Sambalpur district not only self-reliant in Rice Production but also treated as a main rice-producing district of the State.

The IADP has been a 'Path finder' for successful programme.

3) Intensive Agricultural Area Programme (IAAP)

The Third Five Year Plan (1960-65) aimed to achieve self-sufficiency in food grains and increase agricultural production to meet the requirements of industry and exports. Besides, the mid term appraisal of the Third Five Year Plan observed that "Much greater emphasis should be given to the development of scientific and progressive agriculture in an intensive manner in areas where a high agricultural production potentialities". The Government of India formulated the Intensive Agricultural Area Programme (IAAP) with a view to cover at least 20 per cent to 25 per cent of the cultivated area of the country and this area should be selected for the intensive development of import crops such as wheat, paddy, millets, cotton, sugarcane, potato, pulses etc. The programme was launched in 1964-65.

The aim of IAAP was to bring about a progressive increase in the production of main crops in selected areas by an intensive package approach i.e; the use of inter-related factors - physical, social and institutional-in-strategic combination which were likely to exert an impact on agricultural production.

It was decided to implement such programme in the selected blocks of the country as well as the state. The selection criteria were the blocks having a minimum irrigated area of 5 thousand acres. In Orissa a total of 86 blocks were covered under the Intensive Agricultural Area Programme during the period of Fourth Five Year Plan an additional 46 blocks were brought under the programme, taking total coverage of blocks up to 132. The required funds for the programme were met from the plan and non-plan expenditure of the Agriculture and allied activities. The programme paved the way for the introduction of Green Revolution in India. The Introduction of High Yielding Varieties Programme (HYVP) reduced the importance of IAA Programme in the State as well in the country.

4) High Yielding Varieties Programme (HYVP)

The High Yielding Varieties Programme (HYVP) was launched in the country from the kharif seasons of 1966-67 as a major plank of new agricultural strategy under the economic planning system. The important objective of the programme was to attain self-sufficiency in food by the end of 1970-71. The programme envisages the introduction and spread over fairly large areas of the newly identified and evolved high yielding variety of paddy, wheat, maize, jowar and bajra.

The HYVP proposes to make a technological break-through in Indian agriculture which consists of the introduction of new and high-yielding varieties of improved seeds, increased application of the right amount of fertilizers and extension of the use of pesticides so that the crop produced is not destroyed by insects. To enable the farmers to undertake this agricultural practice, the Reserve Bank of India (RBI) agreed to relax the usual terms and conditions in respect of Central Cooperative Banks (CCBs) for the purpose of financing such cultivators.

During the Fourth Five Year Plan about 742.6 thousand hectares of land was brought under the HYV programme in Orissa. This has increased to about 1860 thousand hectares of land during Fifth Five Year Plan with an investment of about Rs. 2 Crores.

This programme mainly confined to good land and to those farmers who have the resources and the adaptability to embrace the progress of technology. This programme became successful in the states like Punjab, Haryana and a part of Gujarat, Maharashtra, Andhra Pradesh and Tamil Nadu in general and Punjab, and Haryana in particular, where wheat is the main food crop. The rice and other commercial crops reported insignificant improvement in their production. Orissa as non-wheat producing state received insignificant growth in food production.

5) Small Farmers Development Agency (SFDA)

The Reserve Bank of India appointed All-India Rural Credit Review Committee on 1969, under the Chairmanship of Sri B.Venkatappiah. The committee in its interim report recommended for the establishment of Small Farmers Development Agency (SFDA) in following words:

"The special efforts proposed are to be restricted to those cultivators who can be developed into surplus farmers if they adopt improved techniques on the basis of support in terms of supplies, irrigation, services of machinery etc. Appropriate schemes have to be drawn up by technical experts with reference to local resources and requirements, so that such cultivators can undertake specific lines of investment (e.g. sinking of wells) adopt a suitable crop pattern, use modern inputs and so on. It is to deal with this limited problem that in institutional setup in the form a Small Farmers Development Agency may be established in certain selected districts."

The important functions of the Agency was to, (i) investigate and identify the problems of small farmers and endeavour to see that the provision of various services and supplies to small farmers is ensured. (ii) help small farmer to secure loans from co-operative banks and other assistance like obtain improved seeds, fertilizers and other inputs. (iii) The agency is to provide various services such as spraying of insecticides, hiring out of tractors and land leveling to small farmers through the agro-industries corporations or other appropriate bodies and institutions including cooperatives and local authorities such as Zilla Parishad and extension services. (iv) to draw up plans for investment and production activities to be undertaken by the cultivators participating in the programme. (v) To explore the possibility of adding to the income of the small farmers by assisting them in taking up animal husbandry activities such as dairy and poultry. (vi) It should endeavour to promote the flow of short-term, medium-term and long-term co-operative credit to small cultivators for appropriate purposes from the Agricultural Credit Societies and Central Cooperative banks on the one hand and the land development banks on the other. The scheme was included in the Fourth Five Year Plan. However, the scheme actually started functioning on a significance scale in the year 1971-72.

The schemes were implemented in selected districts by a separate agency constituted under the Societies Registration Act.

The scheme was financed by the State and Central Government on matching basis. The provision of subsidy was also made by the agency at the rate of 25 per cent to non-tribal small farmers, 33.3 per cent to non-tribal marginal farmers and 50 per cent to Tribal farmers in capital investments and inputs subject to maximum of Rs 3000 and Rs 5000 respectively for any farmers.

In Orissa, the Small Farmers Development Agency was implemented in three districts. They were Bolangir, Dhenkanal and Ganjam. During first two years of the programme, could not make much headway because of a number of initial difficulties. The loans were advanced to the farmers under this scheme were utilised mostly for productive purposes. Orissa stand second in utilisation of loans in all-India basis after Kerala. The State utilised about 83.6 per cent of the loans sanctioned under the scheme.

During the period between 1971-72 and 1980, about 272 lakh families in 115 blocks less than seven SFDA were benefitted. The total loans mobilised stood at Rs. 38.4 crores. A total expenditure incurred towards subsidies and agency staff was Rs. 14.8 crores.

The SFDA was the first rural development programme in the country where the Central Government, State Government and Financial Institutions maintained proper linkage for the success of the programme. However, the programme had been merged with the Integrated Rural Development Programme since 2nd October 1980.

6) Marginal Farmers and Agricultural Labourers Development Agency (MFALDA)

The Marginal Farmers and Agricultural Labourers Development Agencies were set up along with SFDA on the recommendation made by Rural Credit Review Committee (1969). The principal objective of the prgramme is to assist the marginal farmers and agricultural labourers in maximum productive use of their small holding and skills by undertaking horticulture, animal husbandry and other economic activities, like rural industries etc.

The important functions of the programme were to (i) identify eligible beneficiaries and their problems (ii) to formulate economic programmes for providing gainful employment to the participants. (iii) to promote infrastructural facilities for production, processing, storage and marketing of products (iv) to promote rural industries.

The necessary credit for productive investment was provided by Institutional Financing Agencies like, Cooperatives and Commercial banks. Besides provision of matching subsidies were also provided to the beneficiaries. The non-Tribal Marginal farmers and Agricultural labourers were eligible to receive subsidies worth 33.3 per cent on the capital investments and inputs, where as this was 50 per cent for tribal beneficiaries, subject to maximum of Rs 3000/- and Rs 5000/- respectively.

The Marginal Farmers and Agricultural Labourers Development Agency was launched during the year 1971-72 in the districts of Cuttack and Keonjhar. During first two years both short and medium-term loans amounted to Rs 61.32 lakhs and Rs 45.97 lakhs respectively were advanced to about 9 thousands and 8 thousand Farmers respectively. A total sum of Rs 1.6 cores was earmarked in the year 1974-75. This amount has increased to Rs 4.2 crores in the year 1975-76. Under the project 2.6 lakh Marginal farmers and 0.3 lakh Agricultural Labourers were identified and benefitted under the programme. Among them about 70 per cent of the beneficiaries were enrolled as members of cooperative societies.

7) Drought Prone Area Programme (DPAP)

A Rural works programme was initiated in 1970-71 with the objective of providing development investment in drought prone areas. During the Fourth Five Year Plan the main emphasis of the programme was on labour intensive works such as medium and minor irrigation, road construction, afforestration, soil conservation and provision of drinking water. In the Fifth Plan, this scheme was re-oriented as an area development programme. The strategy of this programme was to improve the economy of the areas covered, through a package of infrastructural and on-farm development activities with the objective of optimum utilisation of land, water, human and livestock resources. This programme was also targeted the weaker sections of the society like, Small and Marginal farmers, Agricultural Labourers and other rural poor, who have no assured source of income. Co-operative societies were organised to act accordingly. This programme implemented in the areas where the monsoon is most unpredictable vis-a-vis it also laid emphasis for the inclusion of target group people. Thus, this programme was the first in its category, which included both the area approach and target group approach. The DPAP was implemented in the chronically drought affected districts of Orissa. Considering the concentration of weaker sections as well as drought prone area the programme was implemented in 11 blocks of Kalahandi and 14 blocks of Phulbani district in Orissa. During the Fourth Plan the scheme was fully financed by the Government of India. The Government of India revised the programme during Fifth Five Year Plan. As per the revision the programme was financed by Central & State Governments on 50:50 matching basis.

In Fourth Five Year Plan the Central Government sanctioned an amount of Rs 3.4 Crores to Orissa for the programme. During the years 1974-80 expenditure on the programme was stood at Rs 14.2 Crores on different schemes. The programme has been extended to 14 more blocks of Bolangir and Sambalpur districts (8 blocks in Bolangir and 6 blocks in Sambalpur) bringing total blocks to 39 in 4 districts of the State. The State Plan allocation for the Sixth Plan was Rs 7 Crores against the anticipated expenditure of Rs 7.1 Crores. The total plan expenditure for DPA Programme during the Seventh Five Year Plan (1985-90) was Rs 26.5 Crores. The launching of Eighth Plan was delayed by two years due to political instability in the country. However the programme received Rs 12.7 Crores in 1990-91 and 1991-92. The Drought Prone Area Development Programme is being operated in 47 blocks (2 blocks each in Boudh, Sonepur, Dhenkanal, 12 blocks in Phulbani, 10 blocks in Kalahandi, 8 blocks in Bolangir, 6 blocks in Bargarh and 5 blocks in Nuapada districts) Spread over to 8 districts of the State during the Eighth Five Year Plan (1992-97). The Total expenditure incurred under the plan was Rs 36.9 Crores. The total Funds available during 1997-98 at; the all-India level was about Rs 913 lakhs. The total Expenditure incurred during the year was Rs 436 lakhs. The expenditure was thus 47.8 per cent of the total funds available under the programme. The percentage share of total expenditure to total funds available was about 48.6 per cent.

8) Integrated Tribal Development Agencies (I T D A)

Next to Africa, India has the largest concentration of the tribal population in the World. Though all the states have tribal population in various degrees of concentration, majority of them is found in Bihar, Gujurat, Madhya Pradesh, Maharastra, Orissa, Rajasthan and West Bengal. Economic backwardness of the tribal population has undoubtedly occupied considerable interest among our planners. The First Five Year Plan laid down its priorities for tribal development in three broad categories namely education, economic uplift and health, housing and other schemes. Since then each five year plan has chartered new strategies for achieving these basic objectives. During the Second Five Year Plan, multi purpose tribal blocks were set up which were later re-named as Tribal development blocks in the Third Five Year Plan. Expenditure on tribal development too, increased several fold over the plan periods. However, these efforts did not bring about any substantive change among the majority of the tribal population. It is noticed that, in the first three plans emphasis was placed on sectoral plans under various subjects such as agriculture, industry, transportation, health and education etc. Most of these were conceived at the National or at the State level. The Fourth Five Year Plan gave importance to planning at the district level and to experimental studies on growth centres for evolving a planning strategy at the grass-root level. In this context, the Government of India has sanctioned pilot projects for tribal development in the central agricultural sector. Among the Six projects sanctioned in All-India level, Ganjam and Koraput districts were selected in Orissa. The outlay on each of these projects was Rs 2 Crores. Under the Tribal Development Agencies (1972-73) the Tibettan Re-settlement scheme at Chandragiri of Ganjam district and a Saura Development Scheme in Koraput district were brought out.

A new strategy has been evolved for planning the development of the tribal communities during the Fifth Plan period. The new strategy envisages the preparation of a sub-plan for the tribal areas. The first exercise in this regard is to demarcate the tribal areas based on the tribal population. These are;

(i) Areas, where the tribal concentration of 50 per cent or above.

(ii) Areas of dispersed tribal population below 50 per cent.

(iii) Extremely backward and isolated little communities.

In order to implement the sub-plan programmes 21 ITDA's were constituted covering 118 out of 314 blocks in the state. Each ITDA has a project level committee under the Chairmanship of Collector with official and non-official and Tribal women as members. They have to draw up the plan and programmes at ITDA level and review and monitor the developmental activities of different Department. Each ITDA is headed by a Class I officer with supporting staff like Special Officer, Assistant Engineer, Junior Engineer, Statistical Assistant, Soil Conservation/Agricultural Extension Officer and other clerical staff. 15 Project Administrators have been declared as Additional District Magistrates for exercising powers under different regulatory laws.

There were about 47 thousand villages in Orissa; out of that 18.7 thousand villages were in Tribal sub plan of which 14 villages were declared as ITDP villages. They were spread over to about 98 blocks of the State up to 1977-78. A total financial outlay of Rs 189 crore was earmarked for the programme in 1979-80 with a view to cover about 2 thousand families. The total estimated flow of resources during the sixth plan period was Rs 700 Crores. It is observed that 36 per cent of the total outlay of the State during Sixth Plan Period was earmarked for investment as against 23 per cent during fifth plan period. About 5.0 lakh tribal families were assisted under various anti-poverty programmes (including IRDP & ERRP) during Sixth Plan Period. During the Seventh Plan period, about 7.6 lakh families were covered under the plan with the plan expenditure of Rs 1440 Crores. The plan allocation for the sub-plan during the year 1990-91 and 91-92 was estimated at Rs 391 crores and Rs 590 crores respectively. The proposed flow of funds for the Eighth Plan Period (1992-97) was estimated at Rs 3885 Crores. The Flow of funds during 1992-93 was of the order of Rs 459 Crores. This covered about 34 families. The total funds for the year 1993-94 have increased to Rs 466 crores. Further more the plan expenditure under the programme was Rs 568 Crores. Under the plan 43 thousand families were benefitted in the year 1993-94. Where as this stood at 41 thousand during 1994-95. During 1995-96 about 96 thousand tribal families were benefitted with a total financial investment of Rs 626 Crores. The total plan out lay for the year 1996-97 and 1997-98 was Rs 862 Crores and Rs 749 Crores respectively.

9) Modified Area Development Approach (MADA)

Article 46 of the constitution enjoins up on the State to promote with special care the educational and economic interest of the weaker sections and in particular Scheduled Castes and Scheduled Tribes and to protect them from social injustice and all forms of exploitation. The approach for development of Scheduled Tribes was first laid down by the first Prime Minister of India, Late Pandit Jawaharlal Nehru in his "Tribal Panchseel" more particularly emphasised on the preservation of tribal culture. The Tribal Sub-plan approach was operated in mid seventies. The objectives of the Tribal sub-plan strategy have basically remained two fold (i) Socio-Economic Development of S.Ts. and (ii) Protection of tribals against exploitation. Integrated Tribal Development Programmes in the form of Integrated Tribal Development Agencies (I T D A) were implemented in the areas where the concentration of tribal population is more than 50 per cent, and they live in extremely backward areas. For the all-round development of the Tribals outside the Sub-plan areas a new programme called Modified Area Development Approach (MADA) was launched in 1978-79. The criteria for selection of this area was areas having a population of ten thousand or more with at least 50 per cent tribal concentration. The identified areas called as MADA Pockets. In these pockets individual family-oriented schemes as well as community benefit oriented programmes are to be implemented. There is a MADA level Advisory Committee for each MADA Sub-Collector concerned with officials and non-officials like peoples representatives as members. This Advisory Committee is responsible for drawn up programmes and overseas the implementation.

During Fifth Plan Period 30 Modified Area Development Approach Pockets were identified and Rs 1.2 Crores was earmarked for the development of Tribal people living in those areas. The number of pocket has increased to 37 during Six Plan period. A Total sum of Rs 5.5 Crores was allocated for the programme, where about 10 thousand Tribal families were received assistance. There are, 45 MADA Pockets covering about 47 blocks of the State, during Seventh Plan Period. The total amount of Rs 7.2 Crores was earmarked for the implementation of different schemes. Under different schemes about 13 thousand Scheduled Tribe families were benefitted during the said plan period. In two annual plans i.e; 1990-91, and 1991-92 about Five thousand families benefitted under the programme. The total investment of Rs 2.2 crores and Rs 2.5 crores were made for the year 1990-91 and 1991-92 respectively. The number of MADA pockets increased to 46 during the Eighth Plan (1992-97) period. A total Fund of Rs 16.4 crores was utilitised for implementation of different programmes in the MADA Pockets. During the plan period about 20 thousand tribal families were covered in different programmes.

10) Command Area Development Programme (CADP)

The Command Area Development Programme was introduced in the Country in 1974-75 with a view to realising a fast and optimum utilisation of the irrigation potential created in the major irrigation projects. In Orissa, the programme was launched in 1976-77 covering 52 blocks in the districts of Cuttack, Puri, Balasore, Sambalpur and Bolangir. It was spread over to about 5.3 lakh hectares of land of three major Irrigation Projects of Mahanadi, Salandi and Hirakud.

The basic concept of the Programme was to step up agricultural production by optimum utilisation of water by controlled irrigation and adoption of multi-cropping pattern on an extensive scale. The components of C A D Project which are given highest priority in realising these objectives are, (i) Construction of field channels (ii) Warabandi i.e; regulated and assured water supply to the farmers (iii) Consolidation and (iv) Adoption of Multi-cropping pattern. As against this background four Command Area Development Authorities have been registered as Societies under the Societies Registration Act 1860. Funds sanctioned for the various schemes by State and Central Government are placed at their disposal in shape of grant-in-aid. A special loan account was also set up by the ARDC with 50% contribution from Central Government and 25% each by the State Government and ARDC to finance on-farm development works for the ineligible and unwilling beneficiaries.

During the Fifth Plan the major achievement was,

conducting of a large number of multi-crop demonstrations to make the farmers aware of the needs for having three cropping patterns. Small and Marginal farmers were also involved themselves in the programme and became members of Co-operative Societies. A modest beginning was also made in demonstration of proper water Management by Construction of field channels to serve about 3 thousand hectares of land. A total financial provision of Rs 12.5 Crores was made for the programme.

The principle components of the Command Area Development Programme during the Sixth Five Year Plan (1980-85) have been (i) Construction of field channels including field drains (ii) Topographical Survey (iii) Soil Conservation and Survey (iv) Rotational water supply to the beneficiary farmers (v) Multiple Crop Demonstration, including mini-kits and farmers training.

During the said plan period about 1.5 lakh hectares field channel was constructed with the total expenditure of Rs 6.9 Crores.

The Command Area Development Programme expanded to 58 blocks in the districts of Cuttack, Puri, Balasore, Sambalpur, Bolangir and Koraput. An area of 2.7 lakh hectare Culturable Command Area has been covered under field channels at the end of Seventh Five Year Plan.

The Principal Component of CAD Programme during the Eighth Five Year Plan (1992-97) was (i) Survey Planning and Design (ii) Construction of field channels, drains and land leveling (iii) Rotational water supply (iv) Adaptive Trails (v) Farmers participation (vi) Training (vii) Conjunctive use of surface and ground water (viii) Marketing and Communication and (ix) Monitoring and evaluation.

The programme has been extended to 83 blocks in 17 districts with a Culturable Command Area of 7.4 lakh hectares during Eighth Plan Period. A total sum of Rs 18.4 Crores was spending under the programme during said plan period.

Table – 1

Achievement under Command Area Development Programme (At all-India level)

(In Million ha)

Year	*Construction of field channels*	*Land Leveling*	*Warabandi*
Seventh Plan			
(1985-90)	11.14	1.93	4.96
1990-91	0.55	0.03	0.58
1991-92	N.A	N. A	N.A
1992-93	0.33	0.03	0.64
1993-94	0.35	0.04	0.51
1994-95	0.30	0.01	0.51
1995-96	0.37	0.02	0.45
1996-97	0.40	0.04	0.64

Source: Annual Plan 1996-97, Planning Commission.

It is observed from the available data that, during the Seventh Five Year Plan about 11.14 million hectares field channels were constructed. About 1.93 million hectare of land leveling activities and 4.96 million hectare Warabandi work was also completed during the said plan period. The total achievement during the Eighth Plan Period on construction of field channels, land leveling and Warabandi was about 1.75 M.ha, 0.14 M.ha, and 2.75 M.ha respectively. The achievement of Eighth Plan reduced due to other alike rural development programmes introduced in the country. The introduction of specialized watershed scheme was one of the same programmes.

11) 20 - Point Programme

The 20-point Economic Programme was announced on 1st July 1975. This programme has three particular aims, these are;

(1) To ensure Social Justice

(2) To relieve Unemployment

(3) To eradicate poverty

Under this programme priority areas were identified, which required positive and immediate action. The 20-point programme did not replace or supplant the Fifth Plan. It only assigned special assistance to limited number of urgent programmes for economic and social reform which did not disturb the basic priorities of the plan. Many of the items of the 20-point programme fall within the perview of State sector. The salient feature of the 20-point programme were;

(1) Meeting the challenges in the price front.

(2) Effective land Reforms and distribution of surplus land among the landless.

(3) Home-sites to Landless Labourers.

(4) Banning of Bonded labour.

(5) Liquidation of Rural Indebtedness.

(6) Enhanced Minimum wages for Agricultural labourers.

(7) Expansion of Irrigation Facilities.

(8) Greater supply of Electric Power.

(9) Special Measures for Development of Handlooms.

(10) More Adequate Supply of Controlled cloth.

(11) Regulation of Private ownership of Urban Land.

(12) Checking Tax Evasion in respect of Urban Property.

(13) Intensification of measures to prevent smuggling.

(14) Liberalisation of Industrial Licenses.

(15) Greater participation by workers in Industrial Management.

(16) National permits for Road Transport operators.

(17) Income Tax exemption for people with Moderate Incomes.

(18) Relief for poor students who reside in hotels outside statutory rationing areas.

(19) Provision of Textbooks and writing materials to students at concessional rates.

(20) Widening the scope of the Apprenticeship Act.

During its first phase period between 1975 to 1977 have directly or indirectly helped the rural poor. Furthermore, during the Janata Government rule between 1977-79 the programme was shelved. This programme was once again came to the forefront of action with the return of Congress Government to power in 1980. The Commercial Bank was directed to implement the 20-point programme. The programme was restructured on August 20; 1986 and came into implementation from April 1 1987. The avowed objective of the comprehensive new programme has been to eradicate poverty and create full employment. The salient features of the revised programme are;

(1) Attack on Rural Poverty (2) Promotion of rain fed agriculture (3) Better use of irrigation water (4) Bigger harvest (5) Enforcement of land reforms (6) Special programmes for rural labour (7) Clean drinking water (8) Health for all (9) Two-child norms (10) Expansion of education (11) Justice to Scheduled Castes and Tribes (12) Equality for women (13) New opportunity for youth (14) Housing for the people (15) Improvement of slums (16) New strategy for forestry (17) Protection of environment (18) Concern for the consumer (19) Energy for the village and (20) A responsive Administration.

The revised 20-Point Programme seeks to achieve four major objectives as; (1) To check inflation and ensures adequate supply of essential commodities (2) To uplift the downtrodden sections of the Society by providing them economic and social justice. (3) To protect consumers (4) to offer responsible and co-operative administration.

The new 20-Point Programme is intended for the amelioration of the economic conditions of the weaker sections of the society. The State Orissa has taken adequate care to implement the programme effectively throughout the state. Particular care has been taken to allocate adequate Funds in the budget every year for different schemes under 20-Point Programme. During the Sixth Plan Period more than 85 per cent of the plan allocation have been provided for the purpose.

The State Government has set up Monitoring Committees at different level and the programmes are reviewed by the officials and non-officials in different forums starting from the block to the State level. The committees set up at different level take stock of the manner of implementation of the programmes and suggest remedial measures to remove the operational constraints in the field. Each district has been placed incharge of a member of the Council of Ministers so that the implementation of the various programmes can be monitored indepth through the District Level Committee under his Chairmanship. Recognising the fact that the people's participation is most important in effective implementation of the programmes at the grass-root level, the State Government have associated people's representative in various Committees set up at different levels for review of 20-point programme. Most of the development programmes under 20-point programme were implemented along with other developmental programmes like IRDP, ERRP, NREP, and RLEGP etc.

However, during Sixth Five Year Plan (1980-85) the achievement under 20-Point Programme was as follows:

1) About 17.4 lakh hectares of irrigation potential was created from different irrigation projects.

2) In the State, about 1.3 lakh areas of land have been distributed among 1-lakh beneficiaries.

3) The minimum wages for agricultural labourers have been raised from Rs 4/- per day in 1980 to Rs 7.50 per day.

4) About, 2 thousand bonded labourers were rehabilitated.

5) In the state about 40 thousand tube-wells and 10 thousand sanitary wells were installed.

6) During the plan period about 10 thousand houses were constructed by spending Rs 3 Crores and distributed to homestead less family.

7) In the state about 6.5 thousand additional villages were electrified.

8) Under Family Planning Programme about 6.5 lakh sterilization was made. As a measure of incentive, the State Government has introduced a scheme of awards for their field workers. The "Green Card" system has also been introduced to provide incentive to the employees, who voluntarily accept terminal methods of family planning.

9) Universal Health Care facilities were extended under the programme during the plan period about 25 thousand leprosy patients was treated and equal number of TB cases was treated. Steps were also taken to control blindness.

10) Non-formal education centres and non-formal education centre exclusively for girls were also implemented.

During the Sixth Plan Period about 20 thousand fair price shops were opened for the betterment of public distribution system.

About 2.5 lakh Artisan units with an investment of Rs 25.6 Crores were established during the said plan period.

To improve the quality of working of public enterprises & the State Government established 31 public sector undertakings and two co-operative corporations. Besides, the Government reorganised other public sector undertakings.

Government of India has issued specific guidelines from time to time for effective implementation of the objectives of the programme so that the goals can be achieved within the stipulated time period. As per the guidelines different committees have been constituted at various levels to review the implementation of the programme in the grass root level.

1. State level committee for review of Implementation of Plan Programme.
2. Committee of officers for review of implementation of Plan Programmes.
3. District level committee.
4. Sub-divisional level committee.
5. Block level committee.

Realising the importance of Voluntary Organisations in the effective Implementation of this programme, consultative committees on Voluntary Organisations have also been constituted at state and district level.

Basing on the assessment criteria, state-wise performance score card was compiled by the Ministry of Programme Implementation, Government of India, Orissa stood at second position during 1987-88 and 1988-89, seventh during rest of the years of Seventh Five Year Plan.

During different years of the Eighth Five Year Plan, Orissa secured 12th, 8th, 11th and 4th position in the years 1992-93, 93-94, 94-95 and 95-96 respectively.

In order to accelerate the performance at the field level, district wise assessment of performance under selected items of 20-Point Programme is also made at the State level following the assessment criteria adopted by Government of India.

12) Minimum Needs Programme (MNP)

The concept of Minimum needs accepts the view that there is some nationally accepted norms of social services, which should be provided to all classes of people within a time, bound programme. The provision of free or subsidised services through public agencies is expected to improve the consumption levels of those below the poverty line. Apart from social justice, improved consumption may be expected to contribute to the productive efficiency of the rural and urban workers. This programme was included in Fifth Five Year Plan as an investment on human resources development. The programme resulted from the experience of earlier plans that plan outlays on Social Services were given low priority and were reduced in situations of resources scarcity. It was also experienced that benefits of social services failed to reach the Weaker Sections without conscious effort to that end. There were also Inter-and Intra-regional disparities in social consumption resulting from differences in outlays. The Fifth Plan therefore introduced a Minimum Need Programme (MNP) with the following components.

1. Elementary and adult education.
2. Rural Health.
3. Rural water supply.
4. Rural Roads.
5. Rural Electrification.
6. Housing assistance to rural landless labourers.
7. Environmental improvement of urban slums.
8. Nutrition.

The programme was also launched in Orissa during the Fifth Plan Period. The important objective of the plan was to increase the consumption standard of the lowest 30 per cent of the population. Since such consumption could be partly private and partly social, the National Programme of Minimum Needs assumed considerable importance. Total Funds for Minimum Needs Programme was Rs 216.1 Crores during Fifth Plan. This accounted for about 25.8 per cent of the total plan outlay for the said plan.

During Fifth Plan Period about 6 thousand villages were

electrified and 4.5 thousand irrigation pumps were energised. The Fifth Plan followed by two annual plans i, e; 1978-79 and 1979-80 where about 3 thousand villages were electrified and 6 thousand irrigation pumps were installed. Under the revised MNP, about 323 roads covering 3,586 kilometres were completed during the mentioned period. The enrollment of students in Primary and Middle School during the period from 1974 to 1980 has increased about more than 100 per cent and 150 per cent respectively. After adoption of Minimum Needs Programme the health services of the State has also received utmost attention. As a part of MNP 77 selected PHCs were upgraded to 30 bedded rural hospitals, besides, 942 sub-centres, 1100 family welfare centres were established and about 131 PHC out of 309 PHCs buildings were electrified. About 10 thousand villages were provided drinking water facilities by either tube-wells or sanitary wells. Under MNP about 8 thousand acres of land were distributed to about 162 lakh families (@ 0.04 acres per family) Besides, about 13 thousand houses were constructed. Under the improvement of urban slums scheme 51 thousand inhabitants of the weaker sections were received benefits. It is also observed that 2.5 lakh beneficiaries were provided with local food under the MNP.

In the Sixth Plan (1980-85), it has been mentioned that the programmes under MNP will have to taken as a package and related to specific areas and beneficiary groups. In order to meet this approach the Minimum Needs Programme have been revised as

(1) The landless labourers to be provided with house sites along with financial help for building their own houses is to be extended for urban areas.

(2) To provide safe drinking water facilities to all the villages.

(3) The coverage of mid-day meal scheme for under nourished children and supplementary nutrition programme for mothers and infants to be expanded to the block which have high concentration of

Scheduled Castes, Scheduled Tribes and of people below the poverty line.

The enrolment of children in schools gathered importance as the National Policy on Education seeks to provide free and compulsory education to all children up to 14 years of age. In this respect, the Sixth Plan target of 39.4 lakh children was fully achieved. About 2 lakh people were enrolled in about 6.9 thousand centres under adult education programme. Under the programme 20 PHCs were opened, 17 PHCs were upgraded, about 100 Subsidiary Health Centres (SHCs) were converted to dispensaries and about 23 hundred health sub-centres were also established.

During the plan period about 40 thousand tube-wells and 10 thousand sanitary wells were installed under MNP.

In the State 2.6 thousand Kms of MNP roads were completed and 6.5 thousand villages were electrified.

The programme was also proposed to provide house sites to landless labourers. In this programme about 17 thousand houses were constructed for the purpose. During the plan period about 20.3 lakh beneficiaries were benefitted under nutrition programme with the due assistance of Care and World Food Programme.

In the Seventh Five Year Plan (1985-90), 4 additional items were added in the ongoing Minimum Needs Programme. They are (i) Rural fuel wood plantation (ii) Improved chullah (iii) Public distribution system and (iv) Rural sanitation. Thus, the revised MNP operated with a total of 12 components, since Seventh Plan Period.

In the state, 6 thousand villages were electrified with an investment of Rs39.4 Crores during Seventh Five Year Plan. An area of about 37 thousand hectares of land was planted under rural fuel wood plantation programme with an expenditure of Rs 15 Crores. During the Seventh Five Year Plan with the funds provided from 8th and 9th Finance Commission Awards 8 thousand schools have provided with puccca buildings besides, ten lakh persons were made literate under adult education programme. It is reported that 500 additional PHCs, 50 Community Health Centres and about 2 thousand sub-centres were established during Seventh Plan Period with an expenditure of Rs 25 Crores. About Rs 54.2 Crores of were spending under the rural drinking water supply programme. By the end of the plan period about 36 thousand problem villages were supplied with drinking water facilities either by tube-wells or sanitary wells. The rural sanitation scheme has been implemented through Panchayat Raj department. About 18.5 thousand household latrines, 2 hundred Anganwadi and 6 hundred schools latrines were constructed during seventh plan period with an investment of Rs 0.9 Crores. Environmental improvement of Urban Slums aim at providing important basic amenities such as water supply, street light, road, drain, community bath and latrines and proper swerage system etc. Under this scheme, about 70 thousand slum dwellers were benefitted during the plan period. During the Seventh Five Year Plan period a total expenditure under Nutrition Programme stood at Rs 17.1 Crores.

The Minimum Needs Programme, which was revised during Seventh Five Year Plan, was also continued in the Eighth Five Year Plan (1992-97). However, on July 96 a conference of the Chief Ministers was held on Basic Minimum Services (BMS). The conference has unanimously recommended the adoption of following objectives;

(1) 100 per cent coverage of provision of safe drinking water in rural and urban areas.

(2) 100 per cent coverage of Primary Health Service facilities in rural and urban areas.

(3) Universalisation of Primary Education.

(4) Provision of Public Housing assistance to all shelterless poor families.

(5) Extension of Mid-day Meal in Primary schools to all rural blocks and urban slums.

(6) Provision of connectivity to all unconnected villages and habitants.

(7) Streamline the Public Distribution System with focus upon the poor.

During the Eighth Plan period following physical targets were achieved with an expenditure of Rs 927.7 Crores.

1.	(i)	Enrolment of Child (6-14yrs)	-	16.5 thousand
	(ii)	Enrolment in Adult Education (15-35yrs)	-	64 lakhs
2.		Rural Health		
	(i)	PHCs established		160 nos.
	(ii)	CHCs established		7 nos.
3.		Rural Water Supply		
	(i)	Tube-wells installed	=	10 thousand
	(ii)	Sanitary wells installed	=	6 hundred
4.		Rural Housing beneficiaries	=	40 thousand
5.		Rural electrification	=	1 thousand villages
6.		Slum-dwellers covered under Environmental Improvement Urban slums	=	54 thousand
7.		Nutrition Programme (i) Children beneficiaries	=	30 lakhs
		(ii) Women beneficiaries	=	7 lakhs
8.		Rural Sanitation		
		(1) Community latrines constructed	=	8 nos.
		(2) Institutional latrines constructed	=	7.5 hundred
		(3) Household latrines constructed	=	64 thousand
9.		PDS fair price shops opened	=	8.5 hundred

13) Food For Work Programme:(FFW)

The Food For Work Programme was launched in April 1977. The programme aims at generation of additional employment opportunities in rural areas and creation of durable community assets, which would strengthen the rural infrastructure. The workers were paid in food grains for the job performed by them. The important feature of the programme was;

(i) Provision of a scheme of projects and a list of standards and specifications for the execution of works, besides the necessary organisational arrangements for the assets created.

(ii) Allocations of different States/Union Territories on the basis of 75 per cent benefits to the Marginal farmers and agricultural labourers and remaining 25 per cent importance on incidence of poverty.

(iii) In addition to food grains, assistance in cash to be provided for the procurement of materials required for ensuring the durability of the assets created under the programme.

(iv) High priority to accord afforestration and social forestry and the allocation of 10 per cent of the outlay on projects of this nature.

(v) Another 10 per cent to be earmarked for the creation of assets having a direct impact on the Socio-Economic life of Scheduled Castes and Scheduled Tribes, the development of common house sites, community irrigation wells.

(vi) The amount of wages paid in terms of food grain was fixed at 2 kg per day per head; in addition a cash equivalent of 1 kg of food grains was paid as part of the wages per day.

(vii) Active involvement of Panchayati Raj institutions in the implementation of the programme.

Orissa is one of the pioneer States in implementation of the Food For work Programme. Under the scheme food grains are made available to the State Government free of cost by

Central Government to supplement the budgetary provisions for creating durable assets where the labour component is comparatively high. During the period from 1977-78 to 1979-80, an additional employment opportunity worth 980 lakh man days were generated in the State; by utilising about 4.1 lakh tonnes of food grains and Rs 51.4 Crores in cash.

The FFW programme failed to generate permanent avenues of employment due to the fact that it was not conceived as a part of Integrated Rural Development Programme. This programme was revamped and renamed as National Rural Employment Programme (NREP) and implemented from October 1980. In some special occasions like Draught, flood etc. this programme is also operating in the State as well as in the Country.

14) National Rural Employment Programme (NREP)

The 'Food For Work' programme was restructured and renamed as National Rural Employment Programme (NREP) in October 1980. This is being implemented as centrally sponsored programme with 50 per cent sharing basis between the Centre and States. Additional employment of the order of 300-400 million mandays per year for the unemployed and underemployed was envisaged under the NREP. This programme aims to create community assets like, drinking water wells, community irrigation wells, village tanks, minor irrigation works, rural roads, schools, Panchayat buildings etc. for strengthening rural infrastructure. Besides, important objectives like, (i) Creation of employment opportunities, which aims to provide food to all citizens. (ii) Planned utilisation of manpower for economic development and (iii) an efficient public distribution system for the essential commodities required by the poor was also emphasised. The guidelines further stipulate that 10 per cent of the allocation is to be earmarked for utilisation exclusively for programme of direct benefit to the Scheduled Castes/Tribes and 10 per cent of the allocations were to be earmarked for social forestry.

During the Sixth Plan, the total employment generated under the programme was of the order of 675 lakh Mandays. This Mandays were generated with a plan expenditure of Rs. 64.9 crores, in Orissa.

The Seventh Five Year Plan (1985-90) has created an additional employment opportunity of about 763 lakh Mandays. A total sum of Rs 117.3 Crores was earmarked for the generation of said employment opportunities. The programme was merged with Jawahar Rozgar Yojana (JRY) along with Rural Landless Employment Guarantee Programme (RLEGP) on 1st April 1989.

15) Rural Landless Employment Guarantee Programme (RLEGP)

The Rural Landless Employment Guarantee Programme (RLEGP) was launched on the 15th August 1983 with the objective of generating gainful employment, creating productive assets in rural areas and improving the overall quality of rural life. This was a centrally sponsored programme. This was funded by the Central Government on cent per cent basic. Resources were allocated to the States/Union Territories on the basic of the prescribed criteria. Provision was made to allocate 50 per cent resources to agricultural labourers, marginal farmers and marginal workers the remaining 50 per cent weightage to incidence of poverty. The important component of the programme was;

(i) Construction of rural link roads as part of the MNP.

(ii) Digging of field channels to improve the utilisation of the potential created by large irrigation projects.

(iii) Land development and reclamation of wasteland or degraded land with special emphasis on ecological improvement in hill and desert areas.

(iv) Social forestry.

(v) Social and water conservation works, including improvement of minor irrigation works.

Besides, the programme includes projects of Social Forestry, Indira Awas Yojana and million wells scheme.

The programme came into operation in the mid-year of the Sixth Plan Period, in Orissa, only 73.2 lakh Mandays of employment was generated by the end of the plan period. Due to effective implementation of the programme, it gained momentum as a result, 675 lakh Mandays employment was generated during the Seventh Plan Period. Under the programme 5.3 thousand kilometres of Rural link road was constructed. Social Forestry was one of the important components of the programme about 1.5 lakh hectares of land were planted. In the State 6 thousand hectares irrigation potential was created under different irrigation schemes. Under the programme about 5 thousand primary school buildings and 7 multi-purpose Community Centres were constructed. This programme was merged with Jawahar Rozgar Yojana (JRY) in April 1989.

16) Jawahar Rozgar Yojana (JRY)

Jawahar Rozgar Yojana (JRY) was launched in 28th April 1989. All the ongoing rural wage employment programmes like NREP and RLEGP merged into the JRY. The important features of the programme are;

(i) JRY introduced to be implemented and administered by village Panchayats all over the Country.

(ii) The expenditure for implementation of this programme to be shared by the Central Government and State Government in the proportion of 80:20.

(iii) The allocation of fund to the State will be decide on the basis of poverty criteria.

(iv) Further, devolution of these funds to the districts will be determined in terms of the criteria of backwardness in relation to the weaker section population.

(v) Provision of employment is made to atleast one member of each poor family for 50-100 days in a year.

(vi) A special reservation of 30% for women employment.

(vii) 20 per cent of total resources are allocated for million well schemes.

(viii) At least 2 kgs of food grains per day is given to workers at subsidised rate.

(ix) At least 60 per cent of the resources have to be spent as wage component.

(x) A maximum of 10 per cent of the allocation may be used for incurring expenditure on maintenance of assets.

Table –2

Generation of Employment opportunity & Expenditure under JRY

Period	*Employment generated (In lakh Mandays)*					*Total Expenditure (Rs in Crores)*
	SC	*ST*	*OC*	*TOTAL*	*WOMEN*	
1	2	3	4	5	6	7
1989-90	157.70	205.81	154.12	517.63	107.25	104.46
1990-91	102.62	127.42	111.93	314.97	83.19	128.45
1991-92	105.39	127.99	115.48	348.86	79.78	140.34
1992-93	96.92	119.73	109.74	326.39	88.53	130.67
1993-94 -	139.92	182.13	157.02	479.07	156.18	195.83
1994-95 -	130.78	170.00	142.81	443.59	136.61	187.40
1995-96 -	177.34	218.49	190.21	586.04	187.79	246.84
1996-97 -	96.65	115.09	102.45	314.19	102.77	144.27
1997-98 -	92.47	111.72	95.63	299.82	93.33	150.74
Total	1099.79	1378.38	1179.39	3657.56	1035.43	1429.00
Percentage	(30.1)	(37.7)	(32.2)	(100.0)	(28.3)	

Source: Govt. of Orissa, Economic Survey, 1998-99, P.8/7

It is observed from the above table that, over the period between 1989-90 and 1997-98 about 3657.56 lakh mandays were generated in Orissa. The total expenditure of Rs 1429 crores was earmarked over the period under observation. Furthermore, it is revealed that, the programme objective of special reservation of 30% for women employment has not achieved over the period under observation.

Table – 3

Physical and Financial Achievements under JRY (All-India) During the Period 1995-96 to 1997-98

Year, Physical & Financial	*Target*	*Achievement*	*%age of achievement to the Target*
Physical (Employment in Lakh Mandays)			
1995-96	8480.1	8958.3	106
1996-97	4141.4	4006.3	97.7
1997-98	3864.9	3648.3	94.4
Financial (Rs in Crores)			
1995-96	5791.9	4466.9	77.1
1996-97	2583.4	2164.0	83.8
1997-98	2872.0	2451.7	85.4

Source: Annual Report 1998-99, Ministry of Rural Areas & Employment.

The physical and financial performance of JRY in India is satisfactory, as the Physical achievement is above 90 per cent and the financial achievement is above 75 per cent at the all-India level. The JRY programme emerged as Jawahar Gram Samridhi Yojana (JGSY) with effect from 1st April 1999.

17) Training of Rural Youth for Self-Employment (TRYSEM)

The Training of Rural Youths for Self Employment (TRYSEM) was implemented on August 1979 as a national scheme. The principal objective of the programme was to provide employment opportunities to the rural youth belonging to the families living below the poverty line. The main thrust of the programme is on equipping rural youth with necessary skill and technology to enable them to seek employment, in different rural economic sectors. The target groups of the scheme are rural youths in the age group of 18-35 years from families living below the poverty line. For trades like carpet weaving, gemstone cutting and polishing, diamond cutting and polishing, the age group has been lowered to 14-35 years. This age group was also applicable for disabled persons. The scheme as an IRD sub-scheme was funded by Central and State Government on 50:50 basis. The Central Government have sanctioned a stipend up to Rs 100 per month for the period of training and Rs 50 per month to the training institution so authorized to impart training, facilities.

The Reserve Bank of India (RBI) has directed all Commercial banks, Regional Rural banks and Co-operative banks to associate themselves closely with the TRYSEM right from the stage of selection of youth for Training and include them in suitable and bankable schemes. The banks are also directed to provide finance to the trained youths.

Table – 4

The Following Table presents the achievements under TRYSEM

Plan/Year	*Number of Youths Trained (in thousand)*	*Number of youths employed (in thousand)*	*%age of employment to Trained*
(1)	(2)	(3)	(4)
Sixth Plan (1980-85)	35.7	14.5	40.6
Seventh Plan (1985-90)	57.8	49.1	84.9
Annual Plan (1990-91)	12.7	18.0	141.7
Annual Plan (1991-92)	25.2	21.1	83.7
Eighth Plan (1992-97)	83.0	65.7	79.1
Total up to (1997)	214.4	168.4	78.5

Source: Govt. of Orissa, Economic Survey, relevant.

It is estimated that, about 214.4 thousand rural youths were identified and trained under the scheme, since its inception i.e; the period between 1980 and 1997. Out of the total youths trained, about 168.4 thousand rural youths were rehabilitated during the period under observation. The percentage share of employment to the number of youths trained was 78.5 per cent over the period between 1980 and 1997.

Table – 5

Performance of TRYSEM

(At All-India) (In thousand)

Period	*Number of Youths Trained*	*Number of Youths employed*	*%age of employment to trained*
Sixth Plan (1980-85)	1014.7 -	580.5	57.2
Seventh Plan (1985-90)	998 -	595.1	59.6
Annual Plan (1990-91)	236.2 -	165.3	70.0
Annual Plan (1991-92)	307.0 -	167.4	54.5
Eighth Plan (1992-97)	307.0	167.4	54.5
Total up to (1997)	1517.5	747.4	49.3

Source: Annual Report, 1998-99, Ministry of Rural Areas and Employment.

The per cent of employment during Sixth Plan was only 40.6 per cent, which has increased to 84.9 per cent during Seventh Plan Period. The inception of Eighth Plan has delayed by two years. During that period two annual plans came into operation i.e., 1990-91 and 1991-92. The achievement in employment to Trained was 141.7 per cent and 83.7 per cent respectively in two annual plans mentioned above. During Eighth Plan Period 83 thousand Rural Youths were imparted training under different schemes of TRYSEM. Out of them 65.7 thousand rural youths were employed. The percentage share of employment to the trained has arrived at 79.1 per cent in Eighth Plan Period. It is thus revealed that there has been a wide fluctuation in the percentage of employment generation under TRYSEM. During the same period about 40.7 lakh youths trained at the all-India level. The number of youths employed during the period was about 22.6 lakhs. Thus the percentage of employment to the training was stood at only55.5 per cent at the all-India level, is also not up to the expected level.

18) Self-Employment for the Educated Unemployed Youths: (SEEUY)

The Self-Employment for the Educated Unemployed Youths (SEEUY) was launched in 1983-84.

The objective of the scheme is to encourage the educated unemployed youth to undertake self-employment ventures in Industry, Services and Business through a provision of a package of assistance.

The scheme was expected to cover all educated unemployed youths who have passed HSC and above/non-matric with I T I within the age group of 18-35 years. The women and Technically trained personnel are required to be given due weightage. The scheme intends to provide self-employment to educated youths who are not able to muster their own capital or who have no access to alternative sources of finance. District Industries Centres (DICs) in consultation with the lead banks of the respective areas would function as nodal agency for formulation of Self-employment plans, their implementation and monitoring.

The DIC is responsible for;

- (i) Motivating and selecting the entrepreneurs.
- (ii) Identification and preparation of schemes in trade, service establishments, village and cottage industries.
- (iii) Determining the avocation for each of the entrepreneurs.
- (iv) Recommending loans for the entrepreneurs.
- (v) Obtaining speedy clearance from respective authorities.

The Beneficiaries of the scheme was entitled for loans up to Rs 25 thousand at the concessional rate of interest of 10 per cent per annum in the centrally backward districts and 12 per cent per annum in other districts. Apart from this, the beneficiaries were entitled to 25 per cent capital subsidy on the taskforce attached to each industrial centre. Repayment will be in installments raining between 3-7 years depending upon the nature and profitability of the venture. The amount of bank loan was subsequently raised to Rs 35 thousand during 1986-87. More than 10 thousand youths have been benefitted in Orissa, under the scheme during the said period.

A similar programme for the self-employment of urban poor was also launched on September 1986. This programme was popularly called as Self-Employment Programme for Urban Poor (SEPUP). The urban youths were eligible to borrow for undertaking any production or Service activity. They are also eligible for subsidy computed at 25 per cent of the total amount of assistance given. The scheme is to operate through selected banks. The banker in this scheme is sole responsible for identification, implementation and recovery.

During the reign of Congress government one integrated special employment generation programme called as Prime Ministers Rozgar Yojana was launched in our Country, on 2nd October 1993. The above two programmes merged with the new programme.

19) Development of Women and Children in Rural Areas: (DWCRA)

Development of Women and Children in Rural Areas (DWCRA) was launched in 1982-83. This programme has been implemented in Orissa since 1983-84. The primary objective of focusing attention on the women members of the rural families below the poverty line. This programme aimed at providing opportunities of Self-employment through Training on home-based production and marketing on sustained basis. Under the scheme 10-15 women members belong to families below poverty line can form a DWCRA group. These groups are provided with a revolving fund of Rs 15,000 to take up group income generating activities. The Government of India has enhanced the amount of revolving funds to Rs 25,000/- to outstanding groups. The formations of DWCRA groups have revised. Under the new provision Centre, State and UNICEF will fund the groups so formed in the districts in the ratio 40:40:20 basis. To supplement government efforts the participation of NGOs was also required. The NGOs are required to implement project for providing employment opportunities to rural women. Twenty-six NGOs in the State identified under the scheme. Government of India has started two new programmes in 1995-96. These are (i) Child Care activities and (ii) Information, Education and Communication activities. These activities are to be implemented in all districts of the State. The performance of the DWCRA programme can be seen from the Table-6

Table – 6

Performance of DWCRA in Orissa

Plan/Year	*Groups formed (actual)*	*No. of women beneficiaries (.000)*	*Expenditures (in lakhs)*
1	2	3	4
Seventh Plan (1985-90)	2765	48	438.4
Annual Plan (1990-91)	219	4	64.3
Annual Plan (1991-92)	350	5	63.4
Eighth Plan (1992-97)	5098	71	967.1
Total	8432 (4.6)	128 (4.3)	1533.2 (6.5)
At All-India (1985-86 to 1996 – 97)	184727	2988	23762.7

Source: Govt. of Orissa Economic Survey, relevant issues.

It is observed that about 8432 groups were formed over the period between 1985-1997; the number of women benefited was 128 thousand with total expenditure of Rs 1533.2 lakhs during the same period. This is about 4.6 per cent, 4.3 per cent and 6.5 per cent respectively of the All-India performance.

20) Integrated Rural Development Programme: (IRDP)

The concept of an Integrated Rural Development Programme was first proposed in the Central Government Budget for 1976-77. However the programme came into operation in 1978-79. The IRD programme was adopted as an area based programme with three well defined objectives, namely; (i) growth and production (ii) benefits to the identified target groups living below poverty line of the rural community (iii) Time frame programmes for attainment of full employment. In the initial years, 2000 Community Development blocks were covered under the programme. With a change of Government at Centre the programme has revised and expanded to all the 5011 blocks of the country in 2nd October 1980. The important objective of the programme is to generate additional employment and increase the income level of identified target groups namely small and marginal farmers, agricultural and non-agricultural labourers, share croppers, rural artisan, people belong to Scheduled Castes and Scheduled Tribes and women. The important schemes of development under the programme are, minor irrigation, supply of inputs for agricultural development, land development, soil conservation, soil reclamation and improvement, distribution of Milch and other animals, plough bullocks and bullock carts, horticulture, pisciculture, sericulture, farm forestry, setting up of agro-based, forest-based and village and cottage industries taking up meaningful programmes for rural artisans and encouraging self-employment schemes in service and business activities.

The approach of the programme was based on decentralised micro-level planning at the Block level. Above the block, the formulation of projects and implementation of programmes of rural development was vested on only one agency called District Rural Development Agencies (DRDA). The Involvement of Cooperative banks and Nationalised commercial banks was also emphasised in the programme.

Besides, the representation of the poor in the implementing agencies, at the district, block and village level was also contemplated. The Grant of subsidies for acquiring productive assets by the poor was also continued. The rate of subsidy was at par with the subsidies administrated under SFDA and MFAL programmes. The Central and State Government met the Funds for the programme on matching basis.

The Physical and Financial Achievement under IRD programme since 1980 can be observed from the following Table-7.

Table – 7

Physical and Financial Achievement under IRDP in Orissa

Plan/Year	*No. of families covered*	*%age of beneficiaries*			*Total Investments (Rs in Crores)*
		SCs	*STs*	*WOMEN*	
1	2	3	4	5	6
Sixth Plan (1980-85)	10.3	18.5	21.3	1.1	232.6
Seventh Plan (1985-90)	11.0	22.9	27.3	16.2	303.7
Annual Plan (1990-91)	1.5	24.4	32.3	33.6	63.3
Annual Plan (1991-92)	1.1	27.2	30.9	42.4	71.0
Eighth Plan (1992-97)	6.0	26.3	29.9	39.0	608.3

Source: Govt. of Orissa, Economic Survey, 1998-99.

Over the period between 1980 and 1997 the norms of IRD Programme beneficiaries has been changed. The Criteria of identification of beneficiaries, the income limit for poverty line and the reservations for weaker sections, women and physical handicapped has also been changed over the period under observation.

According to the guidelines of the Government of India, at least 30 per cent of the IRDP beneficiaries should be from the Scheduled Castes and Tribes. It is observed from the table that, a total number of 10.3 lakh beneficiaries were covered during Sixth Plan Period (1980-85) with an investment of Rs 232.6 Crores. During the said plan period about 39.8 per cent of the total IRDP beneficiaries belong to Scheduled Castes and Tribes.

The income criterion for identification of beneficiaries has increased to Rs 6400/- per family per annum during Seventh Plan Period from Rs 3500/- per family per annum during the Sixth Plan Period. In the State, about 11.0 lakh beneficiaries were covered with an investment of Rs 303.7 Crores towards the loans and subsidies. More than 50 per cent of the beneficiaries were form Scheduled Castes and Tribes. It is also observed from the table that the percentage share of women beneficiaries to the total I R D P beneficiaries was stood at 16.2 per cent in the Seventh Plan Period whereas this was only 1 per cent during Sixth Plan.

The annual income for selecting beneficiaries under IRD Programme during Eighth Plan Period has increased to Rs. 11000/- per family per year. As per IRDP norms, the programme should include at least 50 per cent Scheduled Castes and Tribes beneficiaries, 40 per cent women beneficiaries and 3 per cent beneficiaries from physically handicapped category. During Eighth Plan Period (1992-97) about 6 lakh beneficiaries were received assistance of Rs 608.3 Crores. The percentage share of Scheduled Castes and Scheduled Tribes beneficiaries were 26.3 per cent and 29.9 per cent respectively brining their share to 56.2 per cent of the total beneficiaries. It is also revealed from the available data that the percentage share of women beneficiaries in Orissa was stood at 39 per cent to the total IRDP beneficiaries, during Eighth Plan Period.

The total physical achievement at all-India level was 107.4 lakh families as against the target of 65.6 lakhs, during the Eighth Plan Period. It is also evident that about 49.5 per cent SC & ST Families were benefited during the plan period, can be seen from Table -8.

Table – 8

IRDP: Physical Targets and Achievements in India during 1992-93 to 1997-98

Year	*No. of Families Assisted in lakhs*		*%age of achievement to target*	*%age of SC & ST Families Assisted*
	Target	*Achievements*		
1992-93	18.75	20.69	110.3	51.4
1993-94	25.7	25.39	98.8	50.0
1994-95	20.15	21.15	105.5	49.8
1995-96	20.45	20.89	102.1	48.5
1996-97	21.63	19.24	88.9	48.2
1997-98	24.32	17.07	70.2	45.9

Source: Annual Report 1988-89, Ministry of Rural Areas and Employment.

21) Economic Rehabilitation of Rural Poor: ERRP (in Orissa)

The Government of Orissa launched a State level Special Programme for eradication of poverty in June 1980. This programme was popularly called as Economic Rehabilitation of the Rural Poor (ERRP). The important objective of the programme was to assist 10 poorest families per village. For this programme a poorest family was defined as one which has no income-yielding asset of any kind and whose principal means of livelihood was through wage earnings not exceeding Rs 1200/- per annum. The identification of these beneficiary families will be finalised in a meeting of the villagers called for the purpose and attended by the Block level and village officials like, (i) BDO or an Extension Officer (ii) Tahasildar or Revenue Supervisor or Revenue Inspector (iii) V.A.W or V.L.W and (iv) local member of the Panchayat Samiti. In the initial years five sectoral schemes were proposed these are (i) Land based schemes (ii) Animal husbandry schemes (iii) Fishery schemes (iv) Sericulture schemes and (v) other selected scheme. The norms of selection, the pattern of finance and provision of subsidies are different for the schemes. The salient features of the schemes are;

(i) **Land based Schemes:** This scheme had received highest priority. Under the scheme compact patches of Government lands were to be identified and put these for development into income yielding assets through annual crops or plantation crops. The identified poorest beneficiaries were to be employed as wage labourers during the period of development and subsequently conferred ownership rights after yielding income through production. All the expenditure incurred under the scheme was to be borne by Government. It involves no loan components.

(ii) **Animal Husbandry Scheme:** Under this scheme the identified beneficiaries provided with two cows, or goatery, sheep, piggery, poultry and duckery units. Subsidy at a uniform rate of 75 per cent was provided to the beneficiaries. The remaining 25 per cent can be availed as loan from financial institutions. The supply of animals and birds to be ensured by the Government (Block Official).

(iii) **Fishery Scheme:** It was decided to develop and encourage Brackish Water Fishery under this scheme. The identified families of fishermen/semi-fishermen classes to be given usufructory rights. The entire cost of bonding and fixing of wire nets to be subsidised. Public tanks to be leased out and the cost of renovation and cost of feed were fully subsidised.

(iv) **Sericulture:** It was decided to undertake Mulberry plantation on a massive scale. The promotion of Tasar through Arjuna/Asan plantation was also emphasised. The beneficiaries under this scheme are subject to 50 per cent loan from financial institutions and 50 per cent subsidies from government agencies.

(v) **Other Selected Schemes:** Other schemes refer to

handloom and village industries like, lime manufacturing, leatherwork, carpentry, blacksmith and tailoring etc. Under these scheme necessary training for imparting/upgrading the skills were arranged at free of cost with provision of stipends to the residential trainees. It was also proposed to provide subsidies up to 50 per cent on cost of tools, equipments and raw-materials. The remaining 50 per cent are to be provided from financial institution as loan. In case of village industries the capital investment was not to exceed Rs 5000/- per beneficiaries.

In the Economic Rehabilitation of Rural Poor Programme, the Block Development Officer is the kingpin for implementing, co-coordinating and monitoring the schemes. There was a High Power Committee to authorize expenditure beyond the delegated power of administrative departments, monitor programmes and remove bottlenecks therein.

The target for the Sixth Plan (1980-85) was to rehabilitate 5 lakh poorest families under different schemes. As against this only 3.4 lakh poorest beneficiaries were received assistance under the programme with an investment of Rs 33.93 Crores. It is thus; about 68 per cent of the target was achieved during the Sixth Plan Period. Under the scheme, about 30.5 per cent Scheduled Castes and 30.5 per cent Scheduled Tribes beneficiaries were benefited under the programme. This indicator that about 61 per cent of the total beneficiaries are belong to the Weaker Sections of the society. Besides, 1.73 families belong to destitute class and were assisted without any loan linkages.

The Seventh Five Year Plan (1985-90) aimed to rehabilitate about 4.5 poorest families in the State. During the plan period about 5.5 lakh poorest families were assisted under the scheme. A total expenditure of Rs 49.17 Crores was incurred for the purpose. It is revealed from the available data, that the achievement of the plan was stood at 122 per cent of the target.

The percentage share of Scheduled Castes and Scheduled Tribes beneficiaries were 28.4 per cent and 31.1 per cent respectively during the said plan. It is further observed that the share of weaker sections beneficiaries to the total was 59.5 per cent in Seventh Plan Period as against 61.0 per cent during the Sixth Plan Period. The scheme was been discontinued with effect from October 1990 due to its various weaknesses.

The programme was exclusively of States Programme. Thus all-India comparison cannot be possible. Despite of its failure the theme of the programme bears high value. Such programmes need better Implementation and Monitoring. It is observed since long that a number of rural development programmes failed in India due improper implementation and inadequate monitoring activities. Thus, The Planners, policy makers need to give utmost emphasis on these two activities along with the planning and formulation part of the rural development programmes.

22) Indira Awas Yojana (IAY)

Indira Awas Yojana (IAY) was launched in May 1985. This programme aimed at providing fireproof shelter at free of cost to the rural poor living below the poverty line. The preferred beneficiaries are, Scheduled Castes, Scheduled Tribes and freed bonded labourers. The houses are built by the beneficiaries within the prescribed ceiling limit under the supervision of the technical personnel of the block. The beneficiaries are permitted to build such houses on their own house sites in existing habitations. Since 1989, this scheme has been continuing as a sub-scheme of JRY and 10 per cent of the funds under JRY have been earmarked for this scheme. This scheme treated and operated as an independent scheme since April 1996. The per unit cost under this scheme was Rs 20,000/- for plain areas and Rs 22,000/ for hilly and difficult areas. The end of 1996-97 since inception has constructed 1.9 lakh low cost houses constructed with an expenditure of Rs 271.5 Crores. In the years 1997-98, 36 thousand houses were constructed at the Expenditure of Rs 61.8

Crores. During the same year about 6413 thousand houses were constructed at the total Expenditure of about Rs 1345.8 Crores at the all-India level. The percentage share of Orissa to all-India is only 0.6 percentage and 4.6 per cent respectively for the construction of houses and Expenditures incurred under the scheme. The performance at the All-India level can be seen from Table - 9.

Table-9

All-India Physical and Financial Achievement under IAY during the period 1996-97 to 1997-98

Year	*Target*	*Achievements*	*%age of Achievement to Target*
Physical (No. of Houses in Lakhs)			
1996-97	1.12	3.56	317.9
1997-98	7.18	6.41	89.3
Financial (Rs. in Crores)			
1996-97	1426.6	1385.9	97.3
1997-98	1153.0	1345.8	116.7

Source: Annual of Report, 1998-99, Ministry or Rural Areas and Employment.

23) Integrated Rural Energy Planning Programme (IREP)

The Integrated Rural Energy Planning Programme (IREP) has been operation in selected blocks since 1986-87. The important objective of the programme is to develop planning and Institutional Capacity in the State for preparing/ implementing area based integrated rural energy plans and programmes through which the maximum inputs of all types of energy sources are to be provided for meeting subsistence and productive needs of the area. The IREP is a centrally sponsored scheme. Government of India, Planning Commission provides financial assistance for infrastructure and State Government allocates funds for implementation of various renewable energy development schemes. In Orissa, the OREDA (Orissa Renewable Energy Development Agency) being the nodal agency deals the schemes since its inception. The important schemes under the programme are installation and supply of (i) Bio-gas (FT) (CT), (ii) Improved chullah, (iii) SPV lighting system and pumps, (iv) Energy plantation (v) Solar water heating systems (vi) Wind mill, (vii) Micro handle (viii) Solar distillation and cooker (ix) Leaf stitching machine, Leaf cup machine and (x) SOV operated TV. During Seventh Five Year Plan (1985-90) the programme implemented in five selected blocks of the State. An expenditure of Rs 50.2 lakhs has been incurred during the said plan period. In two annual plans i.e; 1990-91 and 1991-92 three additional blocks were included under the programme bringing the total blocks to 8. The Eighth Five Year Plan (1992-97) had included 5 additional blocks under the programme. The plan outlay for the schemes was Rs 263 lakhs. As against this plan outlay an amount of Rs 186 lakhs were spend in different schemes of IREP. Therefore the financial achievement during the plan period was about 70.7 per cent of the plan target. It is to conclude that the targets are not fully attained during the plan period.

24) Employment Assurance Scheme: (EAS)

The creation of employment opportunities has always been an important objective of development planning in India. The relative higher growth of population and labour force has led to an increase in the volume of un-employment and under-employment in the Country. In order to provide additional employment opportunities to the rural poor, the Government of India has introduced a new employment generation scheme in 2nd October 1993. The programme is known as Employment Assurance Scheme (EAS).

The crux of the EAS is that, those who are in need and are seeking employment will get assured wage employment for 100 days during the lean agricultural season. In the initial stages, the scheme is to be implemented in 1752 identified backward blocks of 257 districts situated in drought prone areas, desert areas, tribal areas and hill areas in which the RPDs is in operation. However, the important objectives of the scheme are (i) to provide gainful employment during the lean agricultural season in manual work to all able bodied adults in rural areas who are in need and who are desirous of work but failed to find it either on farm or on other rural economic activities (ii) to create economic infrastructure and community assets for sustained employment and development.

The EAS is open to all rural people residing in the area covered by the scheme but targeted to the poor who are needy and want work. A maximum of two adults (18-60 yrs) per family would be provided the assurance of 100 days employment under this scheme, if and when they seek it during the lean agricultural seasons.

The Expenditure under this scheme, which is a centrally sponsored scheme, is shared between the Centre and the States on 80:20 basis. The central assistance to be released directly to the District Rural Development Agencies (DRDAs). The matching share of the States to DRDA by States to be released within fortnight of the release of central share.

In Orissa, the Programme was introduced in 143 blocks. However, this scheme has increased to 175 blocks of the 23 districts in 1994. Further more, the Employment Assurance Scheme implemented in 250 blocks of 27 districts. At present, all 314 blocks of 30 districts of the State were covered under the scheme. Over the period between 1993-94 and 1997-98 about 14.8 Crore mandays of employment generated with an expenditure of Rs 711.5 Crores. It is observed that, about 3.8 Crore mandays of employment generated in the year 1997-98 with the total expenditure of about Rs 188.7 Crores. At the all-India level about 44.5 Crores of mandays employment created with an investment of about Rs 2718.3 Crores in the same year spread over to 1755 backward blocks of 257 districts. Thus, the share of Orissa to the country is 8.5 per cent for mandays employment created and 6.9 per cent of the total expenditures incurred, during the year under observation.

25) Swarnajayanti Gram Swarozgar Yojana (SGSY)

In India a number of rural developments, poverty alleviation programmes have been planned, implemented since inception of planned Economic development. Some of the rural development programmes have shown tremendous progress and able to achieve required goals. It is also observed that, most of the rural development programmes failed to attain success due to a number of factors. Among them faulty planning, implementation, monitoring etc. are believed to be important factors. The experience shows that, the fragmented approach with a multiplicity of schemes was not focus on the needs of the rural poor in a coherent manner. As against this, the Government of India decided to launch a single programme for rural development. Thus, Government of India along with the Reserve Bank of India has launched a single and integrated rural development programme called "Swarnajayanti Gram Swarozgar Yojana" (SGSY) on 1st April 1999.

The Swarnajayanti Gram Swarozgar Yojana (SGSY) came into force after the amalgamation earlier rural development and poverty alleviation programmes like, Integrated Rural Development Programme (IRDP), Development of Women and Children in Rural Areas (DWCRA), Training of Rural Youth for Self Employment (TRYSEM), and Supply of Improved Toolkits to Rural Artisans (SITRA), Ganga Kalyan Yojana (GKY) and Million Well Scheme (MWS). After the Implementation of "SGSY" Programme the former said programmes seized to function. The funding pattern between the Centre and State is to be 75:25.

The programme aims at establishing a large number of Micro enterprises in the rural areas, building upon the potential and expertise of rural poor. The programme aimed at improving the economic condition of the poorest among poor.

The important aspect of the programme is to enable the

beneficiaries to cross the poverty line within three years through creation of additional income opportunities.

The target under this programme is to cover 30 per cent of the rural poor in each block in next five years.

The assisted families under the Yojana will be called as "Swarozgaris". The Swarozgaris may be individual or in the groups. However importance is laid on the group approach, which is known as "Self Help Groups". Efforts are made to involve women members in each SHG. Beside, emphasis is also given on the formation of SHGs exclusively for women. At the Block level at least half of the groups are to be exclusively women groups.

In addition, the organisation of the people living below poverty line as Self-Help Groups, promotion of saving among the members, proper utilisation of fund's so saved, capacity building for the maintenance of records like, Resolution books, Income & Expenditure of the Groups is also given priority.

Under the programme the Block authority or the officers of the local financial agencies are to make a review of the performance of the SHG after six month of its formation. They are to recommend for the release of the "revolving funds to the SHGs for better economic empowerment of the Groups. After the release of the revolving funds in favour of the formed SHGs the Bank/ Block authorities are to review their performance, and recommend and release of Bank credits in their favour if found viable.

The SGSY seeks to lay emphasis on skill development through well-designed trainings. It also provides for promotion of market facilities/opportunities of the goods produced by the SHGs. Individual subsidy under SGSY is uniform at 30 per cent of the project cost subject to a maximum of Rs 7,500/-. In respect of Scheduled Castes and Scheduled Tribes, however, it is 50 per cent subject to maximum of Rs 10,000/-. The subsidy of the SHGs would be at 50 per cent of the cost of the scheme, subject to a ceiling of Rs 1.25 lakh.

Under the programme, the representation of Scheduled Castes and Scheduled Tribes will account for at least 50 per cent the Swarozgaris. Besides there will be the mandatory representation of 40 per cent for women and 3 per cent for disabled in the Groups.

All the Swarozgaris under SGSY are to be covered under Group Insurance Scheme. The products, animals, birds so purchased are to be covered under required Insurance Schemes/Policies.

The SHGs, under the programme can obtain credit from the Financial Institutions. The Credit Scheme is generally of two types, (i) Direct loan to the SHGs (ii) Credit to the SHGs through NGOs. The amount of loan is generally is at par to the deposits mobilised by the SHGs or twice of the amount. The financial institutions may also sanction credit up to 4 times of the deposit amount, based on the performance of the SHGs. All the Credits granted under the Scheme will be treated as medium term loans and minimum repayment time would be of 5 years. The rate of interest for the loans is to be determined as per the guidelines of RBI.

It is observed that, under the Programme, about 74.6 thousand families have been assisted during 1999-2000 in Orissa. The percentage of SC and ST Swarozgaris works out to be about 20.1 per cent and 24.4 per cent respectively. The percentage of Women Swarozgaris is about 29 per cent in the year under observation.

The total investment of Rs 148.37 Crores was incurred during 1999-2000. The credit component and subsidy component was about Rs 94.41 Crores and Rs 53.96 Crores respectively. The per family investment worked out to be about Rs 19,880/-. The credit and subsidy ratio under the programme is about 63.6: 36.4 respectively in the year under observation.

4
GROWTH OF RURAL ECONOMIC SECTORS IN INDIA

The Planned economic development started in India from 1950 – 51. The planners and policy makers have given top most priority for the rural development. In this respect, a number of Rural Development Programmes have also been implemented in India some of them were discussed in previous chapter. Besides the development of rural economic sectors have been received due emphasis during the plan periods. The discussion on the growth of rural economic sectors in India will throw some light on the achievement of rural development in India.

The Economic sectors in the rural India are broadly classified into the three categories. These are primary, secondary and tertiary sectors. The Primary economic sector comprises of Agriculture and its allied activities. The secondary sector refers to the industries exiting and functioning in the rural areas where as the tertiary sectors refers to the service activities in the rural areas. It is thus; the development of these economic sectors will pave the way for the attainment rural development. In the planned economic development process the planners and the policy makers have given emphasis for the development of these economic sectors. The rural development schemes/ programmes introduced in our country since independence have been revolving in the three board economic sectors. As against this, the growth of rural economic sectors will throw light on the achievement of the rural development in India. This chapter is to explain the growth of three rural economic sectors is India. These economic sectors comprise of Agriculture, rural Industries and the tertiary or service sectors in rural areas.

Agriculture

The Rural economic sector is often termed as natural resource sector presumably because the agriculture and allied activities reflecting the productive system of nature are the primary and predominant occupation of rural people. This sector is primary because it supplies basic necessities of human life, provides basic inputs for industries and in addition to this, purveys goods of exports. India as an agrarian state has been given top priority for the development of agriculture. Although greater emphasis has not been given during the British regime but totally neglected. In the process of planned economic development the planners and policy makers have given utmost priority for the development of the said sector. It is believed that, the rise in agricultural production makes important contributions to general economic development and that within considerable limits at least, it is one of the preconditions which must be established before a take – off into self sustained economic growth becomes possible. It is to say that, the development in agriculture is an essential condition for the development of the rural economy as well as the national economy. The growth of agricultural sector can be examined from few important aspects like, land use pattern, distribution of operational holdings, growth in area of crops, Growth in yield of principal crops.

Land Utilization

The total geographical area of India is about 3.29 million square kilometers or 329 million hectares from the angle of detailed information about the utilization pattern, the area is primarily divided into two categories, i.e. (i) non-reporting areas–the areas for which statistics is not available on accounts of physical and/or political reasons, (ii) reporting areas. The land utilization pattern in India since first plan i.e., 1950–51 to 1990 – 91 can be seen from the table 10.

The table 10 shows that the total geographical area of the country has remained at 328.8 or 329 million hectares over the period between 1950–51 and 1990– 91. The reporting area of the country was 284.3 million hectare in 1950–51. It is thus area for which no reporting was exists stood at 44.5 million rectors. The total reporting area of the country has increased to 305 million hectares in 1990-91. Despite of various steps the unreporting area has not declined significantly. This has declined to 23.8 million hectares or a decline of about 20.7 million hectares. Over the period between 1950-51 and 1990-91 This is all the more significant in view of the fact that the areas which remained unreported are mostly back- ward and assume great importance in the improvement of the life of the people and ecology in the backward areas.

The area under forest has increased from 40.5 million hectares in 1950–51 to 68 million hectares in 1990 –91. This increase of about 27.5 million hectares indicated in improvement by about 67.9 per cent over 1950 – 51. The net increase in the area under forest is the ultimate outcome of the changes that have taken place in the reporting area, the replacement of forest by net sown area, pastures and non-agricultural uses and the afforestration programmes. The net area sown was 118.7 million hectare in 1950–51. This has increased to 142.2 million hectares in 1990–91. The net sown area has increased by 23.5 million hectares which indicates a percentage change of 19.8 per cent over 1950–51. The cropping intensity of the land has also increased from 111.1 per cent in 1950–51 to 130.5 per cent in 1990–91. The table further reveals that over the period between 1950–51 and 1990–91 an additional 53.6 million hectare land was brought under plough registering the net increment of 40.6 per cent. As for as the net area sown is concerned, the additional accretion was limited to 23.5 million hectares i.e., 19.8 per cent. The constraints of topographical conditions of soils, inadequacy of farm inputs etc on the one hand and the restraints effected by an unceasing process of urbanization on the other have been the factors which impeded the improvement in the cropping intensity. However, despite, these banes, it improved if not substantially, but marginally. Besides, these problems, rural industries like potteries, bricks making, quarrying etc are further curtailing the possibilities of enhancing the cropping intensity.

Table - 10

Land use Classification: 1950-51 & 1990-91

(in Million hectares)

		1950-51	*1990-91*
1.	Geographical Area	328.8	328.8
2.	Reporting area for land utilisation statistics	284.3 (100.0)	305.0 (100.0)
(i)	Forests	40.5 (14.2)	68.0 (22.3)
(ii)	Not cultivated land excluding follow land	47.6 (16.7)	40.9 (13.4)
(iii)	Other cultivated excluding fallow land	49.4 (17.4)	30.5 (10.0)
(iv)	Fallow lands	28.1 (9.9)	23.4 (7.7)
(v)	Net area sown	118.7 (41.8)	142.2 (46.6)
3.	Gross cropped area	131.9	185.5
	Cropping Intensity	111.1	130.5

Source: *Indian Agriculture in Brief*, Directorate of Economics & Statistics, Ministry of Agriculture and Irrigation, Govt. of India.

The net area irrigated was 20.9 million hectares in 1990 – 51. This has increased to 47.5 million hectares in 1990 –91. It is thus, the net area irrigated has increased to about 26.6 million hectares over the period between 1950 –51 and 1990 –91. The net increment of 127.3 per cent was registered over the period under observation. Despite of the increase, only 35 per cent of the net sown area are irrigated in India. Needless to add that if higher production growth targets in agriculture are to be attained then increasing the use of available irrigation potential and extension of the facility over larger cropped land would have to be attended to with due urgency.

Fertilizer is a catalyst to the use of other improved techniques for cultivation and improving the agricultural production. The per hectare consumption of chemical fertilizer was only 0.6 kg per hectare in 1950–51. This has increased to about 95.3 kg per hectare in 1999–2000. Despite of such substantial increase in the fertilizer consumption by Indian farmers, the country has to import about 25 per cent of the total fertilizer consumption Technological transformation in agriculture in future would depend upon our ability to create conditions for raising fertilizer consumption. Rapid increase in indigenous production has enabled to reduce the constraints of dependence on imports of fertilizers. It is believed that the fertilizer consumption helps to raise the productivity of seeds, use of pesticides at the proper time ensures against loss of crops due to damage by pest. The consumption of pesticides by Indian agriculture shows that only 2.35 thousand tons of pesticides have used in 1950-51. This has increased to 82.36 tons 1990-91. The consumption of pesticides has increased by about 35 times over the period under observation. Thus, the consumption of pesticides has grown rapidly over the years. Advice from agricultural extension staff in this sphere has played a useful role in the matter of detecting the pest and in application of right type and dosage of pesticides.The trends in progress of farm Mechanization shows that the Indian farmers were utilized only 7 tractor in one lakh hectare of land in 1950-51. This has increased to 710 numbers in 1990-91. Over the period, the use of tractors has increased by about 100 times. The use of other modern farm machinery has also been increased over the period between 1950-51 and 1990-91. Although there has been a noteworthy progress in farm mechanization which has been aided by credit facilities and subsidy particularly in electricity charges, the small size and scattered locations of small have deprived small and marginal farmers of the benefits of mechanization on the other hand most of the benefits of mechanization is largely availed by large and medium farmers.

The agricultural growth rate from the point of view of yield rate, the post independence period can be conveniently classified into two periods such as, (i) Pre-green revolution period (1950-1965) and (ii) Post- green revolution period (1966-1991). During the pre- green revolution period, rice recorded the most impressive growth rate in yield from 7 quintals per hectare in 1950 to 10.8 quintals per hectare in1965. The yield growth rate of wheat during the same period was modest as compared to rice. The yield per hectare in the case of wheat improved from 6.6 quintals in 1950 to 9.1 quintals in 1965. Among non-food grains cotton and sugarcane recorded modest growth rates.

During the second period, wheat and potato recorded the most spectacular growth rate. The per hectare yield of wheat has increased to about 24.9 quintals as compared to 19.3 quintals in case of rice. In all other cases the yield growth rate was either modest or very poor. This shows that the new bio-chemical technology adopted after green revolution was particularly suited to wheat production but was not significant in the other crops. The yield rates of commercial crops have been improving in most cases though in sugarcane the growth rate of productivity has more or less remained stagnant since 1970s. Notwithstanding the rapid growth rate of oilseed yields, shortages of edible oils are increasingly felt. In cotton we have attained overall self-sufficiency, though long–staple cotton for blended fabrics still presents some limitations. The growth of agricultural productivity is the combined effort of the government and the farmers. The Government have prepared a number of schemes/programmes have been supported by plan outlay for agriculture sector. This can be seen from the following table. The Table shows that the plan outlay for agricultural sector has increased from Rs 238 crores in First plan to Rs 13004 crores in Eighth plan. The share of this sector in the total plan out lay (for all sectors) has fluctuated. The sector received highest share of 12.9 per cent in fourth plan period and least of only 3.9 per cent in eighth plan period. The table given exhibits the fluctuations in the plan outlay for the sector.

Table – II

Public Sector outlay for Agriculture Sector

(Rs. in crores)

Plan/Annual Plans	*Agriculture Sector*	*All sector*	*% age share of Agriculture to the total outlay*
1	2	3	4
1st plan (1951 –56)	238	2377	10.0
2nd plan (1956 –61)	275	4800	5.7
3rd plan (1961 –66)	591	8099	7.3
4th plan (1969 –74)	2059	15902	12.9
5th plan (1974 –79)	3356	39322	8.5
6th plan (1980 –85)	6440	97500	6.6
7th plan (1985 –90)	10524	180000	5.8
Annual plan (1990 –91)	3803	64717	5.9
Annual plan (1991 –92)	1735	40172	4.3
8th plan (1992 –97)	13004	335856	3.4

Source: Agricultural statistics at a glance, March 1991 Directorate of E & S ministry of Agriculture, Expenditure Budget, 1998–99.

Rural Industries

Rural Industrial sector is the second important economic sector after agriculture. The contribution of this sector to the rural economy as well as to the national economy is very significant. The main advantage of small and rural industries is that they provide immense employment opportunities to the rural masses. This sector provides maximum support to agriculture by way of supplying its inputs and industrial services, encourage the growth of agricultural production by providing a widespread effective market opportunity. The rural industries sector also aims to catering to towns and cities or even export markets and also earn foreign exchange for the economy. The rural industries sector implies a process through which a host of industries appropriate for rural areas are established to improve the socio-economic conditions of the rural poor. No precise and formal definition of rural industries seems to be satisfactory but broadly it denotes a systematic programme to set-up large number of rural industries so expand the scope of employment of the rural people. However, rural industries refer to a host of industries, which would not only include the traditional handicrafts and artisan industries but agro-based industries, light engineering industries, consumer goods producing industries etc. These industries may cater to the need of the locality i.e., rural people or out side i.e. urban and foreign people. These industries may also be of small scale or medium scale organized in modern lines. The important consideration here is that these industries are to be located in rural areas they are to utilize the available local resources natural and manpower and in the process contribute to the growth of employment and income of the rural people. The rural industries sector consists of two broad sub-sectors such as modern small industries and traditional industries. The former covers small scale industries and the power looms where as the later comprises of khadi, village industries, handlooms, sericulture, handicrafts and coir industry.

The economic history of India abounds in magnificent records of affluent village industries. They flourished through the length and breadth of the country not much on the support of the government but on the support of the people the dynamic entrepreneurship. The commendable position of the village industries in the economy got eclipsed in the British rule. The British government had as a matter of policy, skillfully demolished the fabrics of the village industries. As a result, millions of village artisans were thrown out of jobs and reduced to the position of serfs at the mercy of village landlords. The onslaught had cut the very roots of industries and this made their rejuvenation difficult if not impossible. Gandhiji, Who launched the Swadeshi Movement in early 20s counter- attack the prohibitive economic policies of the government and to infuse the momentum in the village communities for rebuilding of these industries afresh, had many a time reiterated that salvation of Indian villages and cottage industries. This belief which was a bone of contention, is realistic and meaningful even in the present context of large-scale industrialization. However, this sector received utmost attention for development during different Five Year Plans. The First Five Year Plan document has observed "A programme of village industries has to be supported by specific measures of assistance as well as by appropriate state policy. In addition to the emphasis on technical improvements, research and other measures for improving efficiency the primary objective of the policy should be to provide a field within which each cottage industry may be able to organize itself" Besides, the Article 43 of the Indian constitution, which refers to directive principles of state policy states "the state shall endeavor to promote cottage industries on an individual or co-operative basis in rural areas". In the light of the above principles the Government of India has been undertaking several measures from time to time on the basis of experience gained to meet new challenges confronting the industries. As against this background we would like to discuss the growth of rural industries during various Five year plans, since Independence.

The Government of India clearly announced in the First Five Year Plan that the development of village industries was as much a matter of state action as the increase in agricultural production. The first plan chalked out a programme of development of rural industries like village oil industry, soap making, palm gur industry, leather industry, hand made paper, bee-keeping, cottage match industry, Khadi and Coir. The stress on these rural industries in the First Plan was a part of the programme of agro-industrial transformation of rural areas. As against this, the total plan outlay for the development was Rs. 42 crores. The second Five year plan aimed at developing small scale and cottage industries side by side with the large – scale industries. The basic strategy of the second plan was to increase investment heavy industries to build up a strong capital base of the economy and to increase the supply of consumer goods by pushing up investment in the small and household industries. A committee was set up under the chairmanship of Prof. D. G. Karve to examine the problems and prospect of village and small industries. The Karve Committee report was published in October 1955. The Committee recommended one coordinated approach for the development of the rural industries. In order to provide institutional support to the village and cottage industries, six specialized boards were created during the plan period. These are:

(i) All-India Handloom Board.

(ii) All-India Handicrafts Board.

(iii) The Khadi and Village Industries Board. (Later converted to Khadi and Village Industries Commission)

(iv) The Small Industries Development Board.

(v) The Silk Board. and

(vi) The Coir Board.

The Committee recommended for the organisation of industrial cooperative societies for the implementation of the rural industry programme. Under the State patronage and assistance many industrial centers cropped up. The important among them are, sports goods, glass ware, foot wear, leather goods, brass manufacture, handloom, bicycle parts, carpentry and wood works. During the said plan Rs. 187 crores were allotted to village and small industries. Integration of village industries with the rural economy and formulation of the concept of rural industrialization were the two conceptual developments that had taken place during the third plan period. A centrally sponsored scheme named Rural Industries Project (RIP) was introduced. The aim of the Rural Industries Project was to promote intensive development of village and small industries in selected rural areas. The actual expenditure during the Third Plan was estimated at Rs. 241 crores. It was decided to protect small industries from the competition of large industries. However, the Government failed to reduce the competition among these. The fourth plan while admitting this fact cautioned the government in the following words. " The operation of the industrial licensing system has not been effective in preventing competition from the large industries and in providing the required degree of initial protection. Nor it has been possible to prevent concentration of industries in large cities and towns. The Fourth plan placed an accent on the concept of viability as the basic requisite for undertaking any economic activity. The plan suggested for the adoption of intermediate technology on a wider scale as a suitable instrument to ensure the benefits of economic and social objectives. The Ashok Mehta Committee, 1968 set out the concept of viability and provided a specific place for Khadi and village Industries in the industrialization of rural sectors. The estimated outlay in the public sector for the village and small industries worked out to be Rs. 251 crores in the Fourth Plan. Besides, the total amount of investment in the private sector exceeded the target of Rs. 560 crores envisaged in the said plan period.

The Fifth plan rightly mentions. A significantly large numbers of persons already dependent on traditional industries like handloom, agriculture, coir, Khadi and village industries are living below the poverty line. Therefore, the important objectives of the programme for the development of different small industries in the Fifth Plan were to facilitate the removal of poverty and inequality in consumption standards of these persons through creation of large scale opportunities for fuller and additional productive employment and improvement of their skills so as to improve their level of earning. The basic thrust of the Fifth Plan was on arresting the displacement of traditional artisans from the existing crafts providing fuller work opportunities, widening employment opportunities in backward areas and ensuring a level of earning adequate enough to meet the basic needs of life. However, the Government has launched several programmes for the development of these industries. With this view, the revised

Fifth Plan allocated a sum of Rs. 510 crores for village and small industries in the public sector. The important objectives of sixth Five year plan was to create employment opportunities as quickly as possible and arresting the massive migration from rural industries to swell the ranks of agricultural labour or to flood the slum population in the urban areas. Besides, the primary objective for rural industrial sector would be to cover all the existing artisans by the development programmes of Khadi, village and Rural industries and to ensure continued and fuller employment to them in their present occupations. In order to meet these objectives the Sixth plan allocated a sum of Rs 1,780 crores for village and small industries. However the actual estimated outlay worked out to be Rs 1952 crores for 1980-85. This sector have, received 1.8 per cent of the total outlay. A review of the progress of the sixth plan reveals that production in this sector has increased from Rs 33,538 crores in 1979-80 to Rs 65,730 crores in 1984-85 and export from Rs 2,281 crores to Rs 4558 crores during the period under observation. With regard to employment, it increased from 234 lakh persons in 1979-80 to 315 lakh in 1984-85. Where as the output target was exceeded in money terms, the employment target could not be achieved, but there was a shortfall to the extent of 11 lakh persons. The power looms have exceeded the targets set for the terminal year of the sixth plan, the small industries have achieved the targets in terms of output, employment and exports. The performance of handicrafts was satisfactory. The important objectives for village industries during Seventh plan (1985-90) period was (i) to assist in the growth as widespread dispersal of industries, (ii) to increase the level of earnings of artisans, (iii) to ensure regular supply of goods and services through use of local skills and resources (iv) and to develop entrepreneurship in combination with improved methods of productions. The said plan made a provision of Rs. 2,752 crores for village and small industries which is 1.5 per cent of total plan outlay. However, the actual expenditure for 1985-90 'the period of the Seventh plan had been estimated at Rs 3,249 crores. A review of the progress of village industries, handloom cloth and coir yarn and coir products fell short of their respective target. Exports from this sector have increased at a compound rate of 26.57 per cent. In the case of employment generation, the compound growth rate was only 4.43 per cent. During two Annual plans i.e., 1990-91 and 1991-92. The growth rate achieved during the seventh plan is not maintained on account of constraints of foreign exchange affecting the availability of imported raw materials, components and capital goods, credit squeeze, high rates of interest, recession of foreign markets etc. In the new orientation to planning during the Eighth plan, people's initiatives and participation were the key element in the process of development. Greater emphasis was also laid on private initiative in industrial development. Several activities pertaining to this sector like processing of agricultural produce in rural areas, sericulture and allied activities have been identified as critical goals in priority sector. The programmes for selected villages for poverty alleviation through increase in

Table 12

Production of VSIs between 1993-94 and 1996-97

SL. NO	*Sector*	*Unit of Measurement*	*1993-94*	*1994-95*	*1995-96*	*1996-97*
1	Khadi	Million Meters	108	115	124	158
2	Village Industries	Rs Crores	3490	4000	3500	3760
3	Coir Fibre	Lakh Tonnes	2.4	2.5	2.5	2.8
4	Small-Scale Industries	Rs Crores	2,36,525	2,60,000	3,50,000	3,80,000
5	Handlooms	M.Sq.Mts	5470	5600	6750	7200
6	Raw Silk	Meters	15,196	16,500	15,610	16,500
7	Handicrafts	Ds Crores	18,250	21,455	25,200	29,600
8	Power looms	M.Sq.Mts	18,482	20,000	16,332	23,000

Source: Annual Plan 1996- 97, Planning Commission, Govt. of India.

employment. It was also aimed to make free innumerable rules, regulations and bureaucratic controls. The total plan outlay of Rs 2799 crores was envisaged for Eighth plan period .The production of village and small industries during 1993-94 to 1996-97 can be seen from the Table 12.

The production in khadi, small-scale industries, Handlooms, Handicrafts sector increased significantly where as the increase in the production of remaining activities is marginal. It is thus more emphasis is need to be given for the development of village industries, coir fiber, raw silk, power looms for the over all development of rural industries in the country. The generation of employment during 1993-94 and 1996-97 can be seen from the table given below.

Table 13

Generation of Employment in VSIs during 1993-94 and 1996-97

(In lakh persons)

Sl No	*Sector*	*1993-94*	*1996-97*	*% age change*
1	Khadi	14.5	14.0	(-)3.4
2	Village Industries	37.0	41.1	(+)11.1
3	Coir Industry	5.5	5.5	0
4	Small-Scale Industries	138.4	146.5	(+) 5.8
5	Handlooms	110.0	112.0	(+) 1.8
6	Seri-culture	56.0	60.0	(+) 7.1
7	Handicraft	58.3	64.0	(+) 9.8
8.	Power looms	55.0	65.0	(+) 18.2
	Total	474.7	508.1	(+) 7.0

Source: Annual Plan 1996 – 97 Planning Commission.

The data available indicates that, there is a change in employment opportunity of about 7 per cent during the period between 1993-94 and 1996-97. The generation of employment in Khadi sector is negative i.e., (-) 3.4 per cent whereas employment opportunity is highest in power looms sector i.e., (+) 18.2 per cent over the period under observation. It is thus the employment opportunity in Khadi and coir industry is declining for the entrepreneurs, although there is enough scope for the development of such industries. The Government is required to create appropriate conditions for the growth of the said rural industries in India, in order to extend employment opportunities to rural people in general and rural unemployed youths in particular.

Service Sector

The rural service sector comprises of rural roads, rural transportation, rural education, rural health, rural electrification rural communications and other rural service sectors.

Rural Roads

The importance of roads in general and rural roads in particular is rightly stated in the seventh plan (1985-90) document "since the country's economy is still largely agrarian in character and the settlement pattern is rural oriented, roads constitute a critical element of the transportation infrastructure. The rural roads in India mostly constructed under various rural development programmes. Besides the village panchayat, the PWD etc are also responsible for the expansion of rural road facilities in the country. As an important input for socio-economic development of rural India the planners and policy maker have been laid emphasis on the development of roads in India during different plan periods. The Third plan aimed at bringing every village in a well-developed agricultural area within 6 Kms of metalloid roads and 2.5 Kms of any road. The Minimum Needs programmme (MNP) during Fifth plan period had given top priority for the development of rural roads in India. The development of rural roads was also received importance in employment generating and Area development programmes implemented in India. The linkage of village by all weather roads as on March 1994 can be seen from the following table-14.

Table –14

Linkage of Villages by All-Weather Roads (As on March 1994)

Village Category population size	*Number of villages*			
	Total	*%age to the total*	*All- weather Road connection total*	*%age of the total No of villages*
1	2	3	4	5
Population on less than 1000	4,59,465	78.0	1,67,789 (36.5%)	28.5
Population between 1000-1500	58,229	9.9	41,966 (72.1%)	7.1
Population 1500 and above	71,623	12.1	64,633 (90.2%)	11.0
Total	5,89,317	100.0	274,388	46.6

Source: Annual Report 1997-98, ministry of rural areas and employment.

It is observed from the table-14 that about 46.6 per cent of the total village have linked with all-weather roads in 1994. How ever, an estimated 90.2 per cent of the villages with population over 1500 and 72.1 per cent of the villages with population between 1000 and 1500 were linked to all -weather roads in 1994. It is also noticed that only 36.5 per cent of the villages with population below 1000 were linked with all-weather roads. Its is thus about 63.5 per cent villages with population below 1000 still remain inaccessible by all weather roads, as against 53.4 per cent villages for all category population. The main problem of such a situation is that at present several organizations handle road construction and maintenance resulting in duplication of effort, lack of uniformity and imbalance development of the network . There is, therefore need to unify the organizational structure for rural road planning, construction and maintenance so as to derive the maximum benefits from the programmes. The Prime ministers Rural Road Programme is the right step to attain the same.

The rural road Transport is of great importance both for movement of passengers and goods. It is ideally suited for short and medium distances because of its inherent advantages such as easy availability and flexibility of operation adaptability to individual needs door to door service reliability flexibility of operation adaptability to individual needs door to door service. This system provides one of the basic infrastructure facilities for economic development of backward areas besides being the feeder service to rail traffic, ports and harbours, and urban areas. The goods transport in rural areas is mostly controlled by bullock-carts, tractors, trucks, mini trucks and other small transport operators. Whereas the passenger services are provided both by public and private sector. The Passenger transport vehicles in rural areas consists of Buses, Trekkers, Auto- Rickshaws and other small transport operators.

Rural Education

India's ancient culture, civilization and history are a well-documented testimony to the great strength of education, which catapulted the Indian civilization to its zenith. . Education has always been considered as the only key component of human development, the only and greatest liberating force. Hence, traditionally, education has always held the most venerable position in our society. Education was the instrument by which the British sought to maintain and strengthen their economic, political and military domination over India. The British adopted a unique model of educating an elite through a foreign language i.e. English. After Independence, the Government of India has continued with the British Education Model as well as the practice. It is true that there is the provision of free and compulsory education for children up to the age of 14 years has not been achieved in our country. Since Independence a number of educational policies programmes, schemes has been adopted in India. Besides, a number of commissions and committees have also been constituted in India for the spread of education and attainment of total literacy. It is believed that, India live in villages, the spread of education in rural areas received top priority by Planners and policy makers. The Educational Institutions imparting education at different levels and the enrolment of students therein can be seen from the table given. The table reveals that the educational Institutions in rural areas and the enrolment of students therein are lagging behind the rural population, although it has increased since 1951. It is also observed that atleast 32 Million rural primary school age children do not attend school, even in states with high participation rates. Poverty, lack of awareness and sincere appreciation among parents about the importance of children's education, family compulsion to engage children for seasonal manual work on the farms are among the factors responsible for irregular attendance and dropouts. The planners and policy makers have been laid emphasis to wipe out such deep-seated

Table –15

Educational Institutions in Rural India (1990-91)

Sl No.	*Type of Institutions*	*No. of Institutions*	*Enrolment (in 000)*
1.	Intermediate/Junior Colleges (Old pattern)	229 (20.6)	67.63 (5.7)
2.	Higher Secondary Schools (10+2) pattern	9,058 (45.4)	7054.79 (40.1)
3.	Higher / Post basic schools	44,375 (69.3)	15921.0 (61.4)
4.	Middle Senior basic schools	1,29,399 (77.4)	27980.2 (68.1)
5.	Primary / Junior basic schools	4,90,647 (86.0)	54546 .89 (79.2)
6.	Pre-Primary basic schools	8,883 (47.5)	422.56 (36.6)

Figures in parenthesis indicate the percentage of figures relating to the rural areas to the total number in the country.

Source: Education in India, 1992-93, Dept. of Education, Ministry of Human Resource Development.

problems. In this connection National education policies introduced and special programmes schemes were also been implemented. The important schemes for education are, Non – formal Education 1979-80), Operation Blackboard (1986) District Institute of Education and Training (1988), Total literacy campaign (1988), Minimum level of learning (1989) and District Primary Education Programme (1992). Despite of various steps the goal has not been achieved in our country. It is thus required to redefine the education and its infrastructural facilities as per present competitive global economy.

Rural Health Services

Health of the people is not only a desirable goal but is also an essential investment in human resources. The Development and strengthening of rural health infrastructure through a three tier system of Health sub-centres, primary Health Centres and community Health centres for delivery of health and family welfare services to the rural community was continued during the plan periods. The growth of such centres can be seen from the table no 16.

Table – 16

Rural Health Service in India
1970 to 1997

(No. In 000)

Year	*Health Sub-centre*	*Primary Health centre*	*Community Health Centre*
1970	28.5	5.1	N.A.
1980	49.3	5.5	N.A.
1990	130.4	20.5	1.9
1997	136.3	22.0	2.6

Source: Annual Reports Ministry of Health & Family Welfare.

The available data reveals that the rural health sub-centres have increased from 28.5 thousand in 1970 to 136.3 in 1997.

The four-fold increase was registered over the period under observation. The same situation was also experienced in case of primary health services. The total number of community health centres stood at 2.6 thousand in the year 1997. The total number of rural dispensaries and rural hospitals was 11.0 thousand and 4.3 thousand respectively in the year 1993. Besides, there are 0.68 hospitals and about 19.4 beds per lakh of rural population in 1992. In order to support the rural health service centres there are 2.7 thousand specialists, 27 thousand doctors, 4.4 thousand ophthalmic assistants, 20 thousand pharmacists, 11 thousand laboratory and X-ray Technicians, 12.7 thousand nurses and mid wives, 34.7 thousand health assistants and 196 thousand Health workers in our country as on March 1996.

Rural Electrification

Electricity is a vital input for industrial and agricultural development. Rural electrification as a plan programme was introduced in the First plan. It was initially envisaged to provide electricity as a social amenity to rural areas and was confined only to a few states. The importance of this programme was especially recognised during the drought in the mid – sixties, when lift irrigation had to be resorted to on a large scale to save subsistence crops. The rural electrification programme gained special importance for providing electricity for operating agricultural pumpsets to utilise available ground water potential. This programme was subsequently integrated with the minimum needs programme. The programme further strengthened by the formation of Rural Electrification Corporation (REC) in 1969. The REC is playing an important role by providing over 90 per cent of the funds for rural electrification as concessional loans to the state electricity Boards or other relevant governmental organisations engaged in the spread of electrification in rural areas of the country. The progress of electrification in Rural India since Independence can be seen from the following table.

Table – 17

Electrification in Rural India between 1950-51 and 1996-97

Year	*No. of villages electrified*	*% age of villages electrified*
1950-51	1500	0.5
1960-61	21,754	3.8
1970-71	106,774	18.5
1980-81	272,625	47.3
1990-91	485,813	83.9
1996-97	495,508	85.6

Source: Five-year plan documents Energy CMIE, March- April, 1999.

It is observed from the above table that, at the time of independence, only 0.5 per cent of the villages in the country were electrified. This has increased to 18.5 per cent in 1970-71. Thereafter, the increase has been very fast covering about 85.6 per cent of villages with electricity in 1996-97. The developed states like Andhra Pradesh, Gujrat, Haryana, Karnataka, Kerala, Maharastra, Punjab and TamilNadu were achieved 100 per cent in connection with rural electrification. Whereas, this is around 50 per cent in some of the North –Eastern states like Meghalaya and Arunachal Pradesh.

Rural Communication System

Efficient and well developed communication system has become synonymous with modernity and economic growth. For developing countries like India, it is one of the critical inputs, which would determine the pace of socio-economic transformation of society. Telecommunication and posts are the two main constituents of any modern communication systems, this is also applicable in the rural areas. The history of modern postal system in India may be traced back to 1837 when postal services and airmail services were opened in Pre-Independence periods. However remarkable progress has been made in post-independence periods. A number of policies were initiated for the development of postal services in rural areas. Under the revised policy for opening of post offices in rural areas made effective from 28th August 1978, norms have been liberalized, for opening of post offices in backward hilly and tribal areas. A post office can now be opened is a Grampanchayat village, if there in no other post office within three kilometers and non-Grampachayat village with the minimum population of 1000 .The growth of rural post offices in India since independence can be seen from the table 18.

Table – 18

Growth of Rural post offices in India between 1950-51 and 1994-95

(in thousand)

Year	*No. of Rural post office*
1950-51	30.8
1960-61	69.5
1970-71	98.8
1980-81	124.3
1994-95	135.9

Source: Annual reports (relevant issues) Department of posts, Govt. of India.

The above table reveals that, the number of rural post offices in India has increased from 30.8 thousand in 1950-51 to 135.9 thousand in and 1994-95. Thus, the growth of 4.4 times has registered during the said period. The rural population per post office was about 10 thousand in 1950-51 has reduced to about 5 thousand in 1994-95 Besides, post offices the rural telecom services has also received emphasis during the plan periods. There are 17 thousands rural telephone exchanges with 1508 thousand telephone lines in India, according to 1995. In India there are 186 thousand villages having public telephone facility in the year 1995. Despite of these efforts, the percentage of telephone connections in rural areas to total number was only 17.8 per cent as against the percentage of telephone exchanges in rural area i.e. 84.7 per cent in 1995. The villages provided with public telephone were only 32.3 per cent in the said year.

Rural Marketing

Marketing facilities and services are the prime- movers in the wheel of economic growth of a country, for they provide channels for effective and efficient flows of goods and services from one sector to another. Their need is directly felt when centres of production are widely and remotely spread and also when volume of goods and services expand a pace. The rural marketing system connotes marketing functions and facilities obtained in rural areas mainly for outflow of agricultural produce but also for inflow of other goods for consumption of rural people. It is evident that the rural marketing in India mostly controlled by the middlemen like village trader, Itinerant trader, Kuchcha arhatiya and pukka arhatiya. Besides these, there are commissioning agents whole salers, retailers, co-operatives and the government.

The rural markets that have been in existence since time immemorial exemplifies the age old marketing traditions of our country. The rural marketing in the 19th and 20th century was plagued with myriad of malpractices in order to mitigate these, various market legislative measures were enacted from time to time. However, the commencement of the five year plans provided an opportunity for the states to take an active lead in regulating markets by way of legislation all over the country. The market regulation has gone a long way in overcoming the malpractice and streamlining existing markets as well as new markets. State Governments are responsible for such enactment's though the central government provides all technical assistance and facilities. The main provisions of these enactment are:

(i) To regulate products (Agricultural) by making an official notifications.

(ii) To constitute market committee for the management of regulated markets.

(iii) To define the area of regulated market.

(iv) To provide standard market yard.

(v) To conduct/supervise the deals among the parties.

(vi) To provide for the use of standard metric weights and measures.

(vii) To provide amenities such as drinking water, water troughs for cattle, cattle sheds, rest houses , canteens etc.

There have been obvious benefits by the establishment of regulated markets in rural areas of the country. The growth of regulated markets can be seen from the table given below i.e.; table no 19.

Table – 19

Growth of Regulated Markets in India, 1950 to 1998

(in Nos.)

Year	*No. of Regulated Markets*
1950	286
1960	715
1970	3406
1980	4452
1990	6217
1998	7062

Source: Annual Report (Relevant Issue), Ministry of Rural Areas & Employment.

It is revealed from the above table that the growth of regulated markets has been steady and impressive, this has increased from 286 in 1950 to 7062 in 1998. This registered about 25 time growth during the period under observation. Utter Pradesh, Bihar and Maharastra are prominent states where the number of such markets has been larger than other states. It is thus, the distribution of regulated markets across the country has been uneven and operational efficiency is debatable. Besides, this there is also a wide institutional approach to the rural marketing. Important among them is the cooperative marketing system comprises of primary marketing societies, District Marketing societies, Apex marketing societies and National agricultural marketing federation. Apart from Legislative as well as Institutional approach there are a number of agencies sponsored by the Government for the development of marketing functions relating to agricultural and rural produces prominent among them are Central Warehousing Corporation of India, National Cooperative Development Corporation, Directorate of Agricultural Marketing and Food Corporation of India.

5

INSTITUTIONS FOR RURAL DEVELOPMENT

The Rural Development in India is a very old phenomenon. Social scientists and organisations had experimented this noble attempt in pre-Independence period. Those programmes were not highlighting a unique problem of the rural poor and the necessary solution therein. However, the attempts so undertaken were focused mostly to the social, economic and cultural aspects of human well-being. The noble attempts made by great and intellectual sons of the soil could not spread over to all part of the country due to lack of government attitude and patronage. The British Government had never felt the importance of rural development in the country. The rulers felt that, rural development was a part of social welfare, which is perhaps contradictory to the British ideology and policies. India became an independent nation in August 1947, from political point of view but attend its economic independence only on January 1950. After attaining the economic independenc, India started its planned Economic Development Programmes with the adoption of Five Year Plan. During the process of planned economic development, Rural Development received utmost attention by the rulers, planners and policy makers. Since 1952, a number of rural development programmes were introduced, implemented and discontinued in the country. The programmes are varied in nature and approach. Some of the programmes proved to be successful and some failures. The success and failure of the programmes governed by a number of factors important among them are:

(i) Nature of the programme,

(ii) Approach of the programme,

(iii) Finance for the programme,

(iv) Implementation of the programme.

Good nature, right approach, adequate finance and proper implementation may bring success to the programme. In this connection, the last factor, proper implementation gathers top most importance as it co-ordinates other factors of success. This can be achieved through good and right institutions.

As against this background, we would like to discuss the structure and functions of the institutions established exclusively for Rural Development from time to time. These institutions can be classified into two such as, (i) Main institutions and (ii) Ancillary institutions. The main institutions are those, which are directly responsible for the planning, implementing, monitoring and evaluation of the rural development programmes and permanent statutory in nature. The ancillary institutions are those, which are indirectly responsible for planning, implementation, monitoring and evaluation and temporary in nature.

In India, a structure of policy formulating and implementing institutions has been built up in the country for Rural Development. Some of them are at the national level, some are single purpose, some relate to a particular target groups, some relate to area, sector and commodity. However, all these institutions aim at fulfilling the national objectives of economic development in general and rural development in particular. The administrative organs of Central and State Governments involved in the process of rural development are at the Centre of the Organisational Structure. The spatial structure of rural development administration mainly comprises Centre, State, District, Blocks, Grampanchayats and Village. At the Centre, the Ministry of Rural Development is in charge of all rural development a programme including those relating to land reforms, village and cottage industries, town and country planning and rural roads etc. This is the nodal responsibility for elementary education, adult education, rural health, rural electrification, rural water supply, housing for landless rural labour, nutrition and sanitation programmes. The ministry has also responsible for all aspects of rural reconstruction and development. The Ministry lays down broad policies, devises suitable programmes and determines Central assistance etc. In addition to the Ministry of Rural Development, the ministries of Agriculture, Commerce and Civil Supplies, Energy, Irrigation and Industry also perform functions related to rural development. The Ministry of Agriculture is in charge of agricultural extension, Ministry of Commerce and Civil Supplies has within its purview the Development Commissioner of Handlooms, several Commodity Boards and the public distribution system. The Ministry of Energy and Irrigation deals with all matters pertaining to water resources development and irrigation and accordingly has important functions pertaining to rural development. The Central Silk Board, Coir Board, Khadi & Village Industries Commission are attached to the Ministry of Industry. The Ministry of Rural Development, for rural development with proper co-operation and coordination from other ministries. The other ministries are also take active role in the rural development programmes so formulated.

Besides, the Ministries, the Reserve Bank of India in the past and NABARD at present play the catalytic role for the success of rural development. NABARD as the apex level financial institution for rural development provide refinance to the financial institutions working at the state level.

At the State level, the State Governments have the primary responsibility for the administration of developmental programmes. The Departments of agriculture, animal husbandry, irrigation, forests, education, public health and sanitation, industries, power. Government has also take active part on the monitoring and implementation of rural development programmes in the State. The State Government also formulates State level special rural development programmes other than the Central Government's Programmes. However, The State Level Organisational Committee is headed by the Secretary for Rural Development, who is in the rank of Commissioner of rural development is assisted by one Deputy Commissioner three Assistant Commissioners and a number of technical officers and subject specialists. Besides, a representative of the Ministry of Rural Development, Government of India is associated as a member of the Committee.

There are a number of Statutory Corporations, Boards and other agencies providing infrastructural, promotional and supporting services for rural development. Important among them are, (i) Rural Electrification Corporation, (ii) The Central Ground Water Board (iii) Minor Irrigation and tube well Corporations (iv) Central and State Warehousing Corporations (v) Central and State Seed Corporations (vi) Food Corporation of India (vii) The Jute and the Cotton Corporation of India (viii) National Cooperative Development Corporation and Cooperative banks in the State (ix) National Agricultural Cooperative Marketing Federation (x) State Trading Corporations, (xi) The Handicraft and Handloom Corporations (xii) The Boards for Coffee, Tea, Rubber, Cardamom, Tobacco, Cashew and Coconut etc. (xiii) The National Dairy Development Board (xiv) The Khadi and Village Industries Commission (xv) State Khadi and Village Industries Board (xvi) The Central Silk Board (xviii) The State Finance Corporation (xix) The Agro-Industries Corporation (xx) The Marketing Regulation Boards etc. The statutory corporations and Boards works for the implementation of various rural development programmes to their expertise.

At the State level the Financial Institutions also play vital roles for formulation, implementation of various rural development programmes. They form one State Level

Coordination Committee taking the representatives of all financial institutions like, Cooperative banks, Nationalised Commercial banks and Regional Rural banks. Besides, the representatives of various government departments are also participate in the formulation and Implementation strategy of the rural development programmes. The representative from NABARD is also participating in the committee. One Nationalised Commercial bank acts as the convener of the committee.

The Third Stage of Institutional Structure for Rural Development is the District Administration. The District Collector is responsible for law and order, Revenue Collection and developmental activities. In the past, the developmental programmes so formulated by the central and state governments were channelised through the District Administration, known as the District Development Coordination Committee. This committee consisting of the Project Officer, the Managing Director of the Central Cooperative Societies, one/two representatives from Cooperative Societies and a Special Rural Credit Officer. Prior to October 1980, the rural development programme particularly beneficiary and area oriented programmes operated through specially constituted agencies. They are, Small Farmers Development Agencies, (SFDA) Marginal Farmers and Agricultural Labourers Development Agencies, Drought Prone Area Programme (DPAP) and Integrated Tribal Development Programme (ITDP), etc. In 1980 the integrated rural development programme was launched. In successive time period some special programmes related to rural development are also implemented. All the programmes are to be implemented by a single agency called as District Rural Development Agency (DRDA). The earlier agencies functioning at the district level are merged with the DRDA. The District Collector/Deputy Commissioner heads the DRDA. Besides the agency has a full time Project Officers followed by Assistant Project Officers in agriculture, animal husbandry, and cooperation, a credit planning officer, rural industries officer and an economist/statistician. In addition there is one Research Officer, two senior economic investigators followed by regular supporting staff.

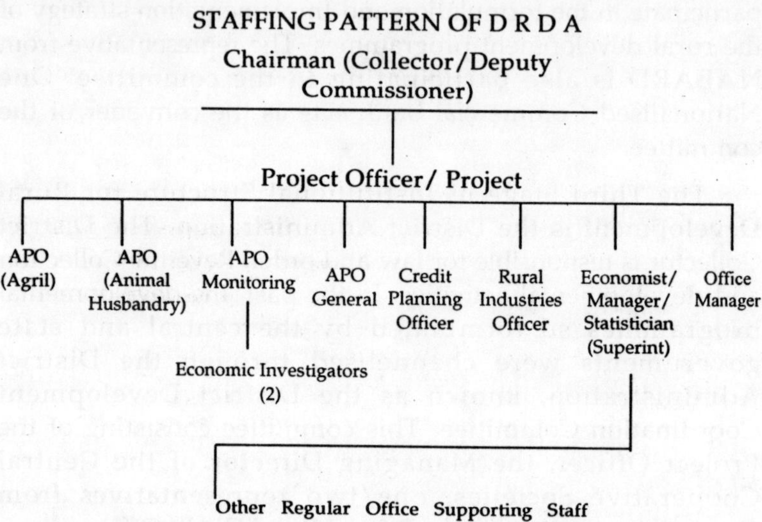

The peoples representatives like, the Chairman Zilla Parishad, Member of Parliament, the MLA and the representatives of Weaker Sections and women are also take active part in the planning process at the district level. The representatives of the lead bank, financial institutions also take active role with the DRDA to formulate District Credit Plans.

According to the Indian Constitution Amendment (74th) Act 1992 The State Governments constituted the District Planning and Development Board to provide necessary guidelines and direction to district planning units and to approve the district plans prepared by the planning units.

The board consists of a Chairman, a Vice-chairman and other members, viz; all Sub-divisional Officers, all Chairman of Panchayat Samities (Block) in the district, the head of lead Bank and Presidents of all Municipal Committees. The Chief

Planning and Development officer acted as the Member Secretary. The district-planning unit comprised the Chief Planning and Development Officer, an economist, a Planning Officer, a Credit Planning Officer and other supporting staff. The position of the Chairman of DPB varies from state to state. In some State a Minister of State Government chairs it and the district Collector is the Chairman in some other.

The Block is the Fourth Important Institution for planning and implementation of rural development programmes. The overall resource situation, to identify human resource situation, particularly from the point of view of employment, to review the ongoing development activities to formulate a package of schemes/programmes to optimize production and augment employment and income, to identify gaps in infrastructure and to devise measures for filling these gaps. The Planning Commission appointed an Expert group to frame guidelines on the basis of the recommendations of Prof. M.L. Dantewala working group. As per the guideline issued on 1978 the block level plan should have the following component;

(i) Production programmes for the target groups in the rural areas.

(ii) Manpower planning and skill development in relation to production programmes.

(iii) A supplementary works programme, where necessary to clear off the backlog of unemployment.

(iv) A programme for the self-employed in the trades and services sector.

(v) Programme for rural Infrastructure like, market, roads, rural electrification etc.

(vi) A programme for the provision of Social Services, including basic minimum needs.

(vii) A programme for Institutional support to the rural poor.

The Administrative setup of the Blocks was defined during

the First Plan Period with the inception of Community Development Programme. With the implementation of Integrated Rural Development and other special developmental schemes/programmes in early 80s, The Administrative setups of the blocks were revised accordingly.

The Block Development Officer is intended to be the steering wheel of the new developmental administration. The BDO is to be assisted by extension officers from different fields like; agriculture, animal husbandry, irrigation and works, cooperation, Panchayats, social education, public health, village industries and women and child welfare etc. Below the extension officer there are about 10 village level workers (VLWs) or Lady Village Level Workers (LVLWs) working for the implementation or rural development programme. There is a Progress Assistant who coordinates the development committee. The people's representatives like; Chairman Panchayat Samiti, MLA and representatives of Weaker Sections and women also participate in the Developmental Planning at the block level. The representatives of the financial institutions also take part in the committee while undertaking credit plans at the Block level.

Village Panchayat is the last recognised institution responsible for planning and implementation of rural development programmes. The village Panchayat as an executive body implements the policies and decisions of the Gram Sabha comprising the entire population of the village. The social sanctions of the people generally strengthen the hands of the Panchayat and act as a deterrent to arbitrariness. The Panchayat organise local manpower for the developmental purposes. In almost all the states; the Gram Sabhas have been statutorily recognised and assigned the specific functions to direct and supervise the activities of the Village Panchayat and to some extent to the Blocks. The important functions performed by the Panchayats are; (i) Civic amenities (ii) Social welfare activities and (iii) Development works. The broad functions of the Panchayat are;

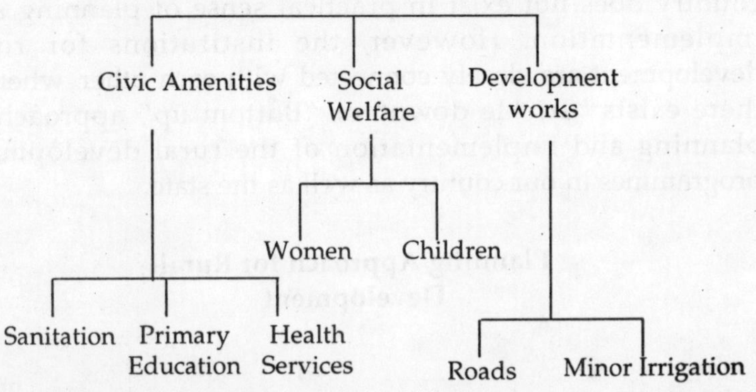

The people's representatives like Ward Members; Sarapanch also took part in decision-making and implementation of the programmes. The village level worker represents the block in village committee. Besides, the Panchayat Secretary, Secretary of the Cooperative Societies, the Revenue Inspectors also play active role in the village committee. Thus village committee comprises of the;

(i) Village level worker

(ii) Panchayat Secretary

(iii) Secretary of the Cooperative Societies.

(iv) Revenue Inspector

(v) The Sarapanch

(vi) The ward members

(vii) The villagers are the General body members.

It is to conclude that, the planning and Implementation of the rural development begins from the root i.e; village and flows upward to the national level. Experience shows that the rural development programme decisions in respect of formulation, strategy & approach are undertaken at the national level and that flowing downward to the village in a "Trickle down approach". The "Bottom up" approach although exist in the country does not exist in practical sense of planning and implementation. However, the institutions for rural development are closely connected with each other, whether there exists "Trickle down" or "Bottom up" approach of planning and implementation of the rural development programmes in our country as well as the state.

Planning Approach for Rural Development

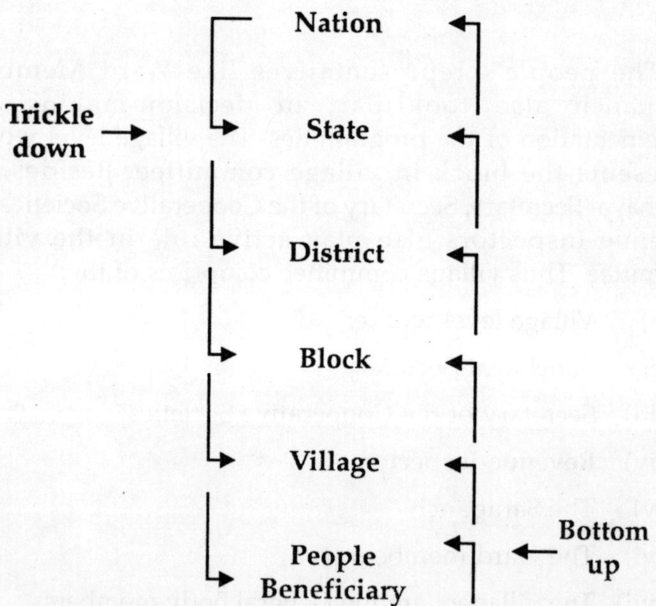

Besides, the administrative set up for planning for Rural Development, there are other Institutions, who plays equal important role in planning, Implementation and Monitoring of rural development programmes. The important among them are (i) the Panchayati Raj System and (ii) the Financial Institutions.

PANCHAYATI RAJ INSTITUTIONS

The successful implementation of rural development programmes requires not only decentralisation of administrative Machinery and Mechanisms for Co-ordination at the local level but also institutions for participation and involvement of local people. From this point of view, the Panchayati Raj institutions play the catalytic role.

The 'Panchayat' or the institution of village councils is as old as India's history and is a part of her tradition. The ancient Panchayats serving as units of local government, discharged most of the functions that affected the life of the village community. There have been a number of indicative citations describing succinctly the forms, functions, features and forces that constructed the strong structure of Panchayats. The erstwhile British Government had caused to supersede the Panchayat institutions by diverting their powers and functions concerning administration, execution and justice, and thereby centralised the administrative set-up to serve its colonial interests. Some of the British rulers like Lord Ripon introduce certain reforms in 1982 and advocated for the revival of the village Institutions. The Royal Commission on Decentralization, of 1909 also favoured the promotion of these institutions, seeking people's participation. The Montague-Chelmsford Reforms of 1919 had given same impetus for reviving the Panchayat bodies. But all these efforts were half-hearted and haphazard making no virtual impact. Gandhiji the father of the Nation was also advocated for the revival of village Panchayat and to entrust full powers for the Independent functions. The Directive Principles of State Policy in the Indian Constitution in Article 40 (Part IV) lays down "The State shall take steps to organise village Panchayats and to endow them with such powers and authority as may be necessary to enable them to function as units of self government." In the process of planned economic development the Government of India introduced the Community Development Programme in 1952. The Government was somewhat doubtful about the achievements of the programme and did not like to rest on the laurels collected by its own officers. Therefore, the Planning Commission appointed a Study Team under the Chairmanship of Balwantrai Mehta on December 1956. The objective of the study team was to review the working of community development and examining the question of reorganization of district administration in the light of new developments. The Study Team suggested a three tier organization consisting of Village Panchayat at the grass root level, Panchayat Samiti at the Block level and Zilla Parishad at the District level. The team advocated the launching of this system simultaneously in the district. According to the study team the democratic decentralization or Panchayati Raj alone can lead to effective rural development. The National Development Council endorsed the recommendations of the committee. However, the Institutions of Panchayat was officially launched on 2nd October 1959.

The Sino-Indian war of 1962, the death of Nehru on 1964, the Indo-Pak hostile on 1965 followed by the death of Lal Bahadur Shastri worsens the financial condition of the Institutions. In most of the States Panchayat election were either forgotten or postponed. In 1977 the Government of India appointed a Committee under the Chairmanship of Mr. Ashok Mehta to study the Panchayati Raj System. The Committee favoured two-tier system of Panchayati Raj in the place of three-tier one as recommended by the Balwantrai Mehta Committee. The Ashok Mehta Committee report had not introduced properly due to the change of Central Government in 1980.

In 1985, the Planning Commission set up a committee to review the existing administrative arrangements for rural development and poverty alleviation programme (CAARD) under the Chairmanship of Prof. G.V.K. Rao. The Committee among other things suggested activization of Panchayati Raj Institutions. In 1986, the Government of India set up a committee under the Chairmanship of L.M. Singhvi to prepare concept paper on the revitalization of the Panchayati Raj Institutions. The committee recommended that the local self-government should be constitutionally recognized, protected and preserved by the inclusion of a new chapter in the constitution. Besides a sub committee of the consultative committee of Parliament under the Chairmanship of Mr. P.K. Thungon recommended for constitutional status to the Panchayati Raj System in India. Due to change in Government at Centre and dissolution of Parliament resulted the delay in enactment of Panchayati Raj Institutions. However, Constitution (73rd) Amendment Act of 1992 became operative on 24th April 1993. The main features of the Act are:

(i) Formation of Gram Sabhas.

(ii) Uniform three-tier system at village, block and district levels with exemption for intermediate level in States with population less than two millions.

(iii) Direct election to all seats for all members at all levels.

(iv) Twenty-one years as the minimum age for membership as well as Chairperson.

(v) Reservation for Scheduled Castes and Scheduled Tribes in proportion to their population both for membership as well as Chairperson.

(vi) Reservation of not less than one-third of the seats for women.

(vii) Five-year term.

(viii) Devolution of powers and responsibilities by the State in the preparation and implementation of development plans.

(ix) Financial arrangements through tax, grant-in-aid; levy, fees etc.

GRAM SABHA (at village level)

At the village level there exists Gram Sabha. Each Gram Sabha consists of all persons registered by virtue of the Representation of the People Act 1950. The persons representing the Gram Sabha or ward areas may preside over the meeting. The members present at the meeting of the shall form the quorum for such meeting and the proceeding of the meeting of the Sabha shall be recorded and authenticated by its president. The Gram Sabha recommends the meeting proceedings to the Gram Panchayat.

GRAM PANCHAYAT (Panchayat level)

One Gram Panchayat divided into wards. The peoples so elected represent one ward. There is a Sarapanch, a Naib-Sarpanch or Up-Sarapanch, the elected representatives of the wards. Among the represent at least one member to represent Scheduled Castes and one member to Scheduled Tribes. Of the total representatives one third reserved for the women.

The Functions of village Panchayat are broadly divided into two categories, which include obligatory and discretionary. They broadly include Sanitation, Conservancy, Water supply, Construction and maintenance of roads, bridges etc. Promotion of agriculture, cottage industries and cooperative institutions, women and child development. Besides their important role is to implement rural development programmes.

PANCHAYAT SAMITI (Block level)

The intermediate tier in the Panchayati Raj System is the Panchayat Samiti, which normally coterminous with Block.

Every Panchayat Samiti consists of

(i) The Chairman and the Vice-Chairman.

(ii) One member elected directly.

(iii) Sarapanches of the Grampanchayats situated within the block.

(iv) Every member of the House of the People and of the legislative assembly representing constituencies, which comprise wholly or partly the area of the Samiti.

(v) Every member of the council of State who is registered as an elector within the area of the Samiti.

Seats shall be reserved for the Scheduled Castes and the Scheduled Tribes depending upon the total population. At least one-third of the total seats to be represented by the women.

The Samiti is mainly entrusted with the developmental activities and is made directly responsible for implementing the rural development programmes. Besides, the preparation of development plans has also been assigned to them. The institution is also promoting economic activities and Social Welfare activities.

ZILLA PARISHAD (at the district level)

The Third and highest tier of Panchayati Raj at the district level is known as Zilla Parishad. The Zilla Parishad consists of:

(a) One member elected directly on the basis of adult suffrage from every constituency with due representation of Scheduled Castes, Scheduled Tribes and women.

(b) Chairman of each Samiti situated within the district.

(c) Every member of the House of the people and of the State legislative assembly representing constituencies, which comprise wholly or partly the area of the Parishad.

(d) Members of the Council of States who are registered as electors within the area of the Parishad.

(e) The Parishad headed by a Chairman/President elected from the members.

(f) The second functionary of the Parishad is the Vice-Chairman/Vice-President to be elected by the members.

The functions of Zilla Parishad include distribution of funds, Preparation of Plans, Projects, Schemes for rural development, Provision and maintenance of schools, Primary health centres, veterinary aid etc. The Parishad act as a connecting bridge between higher planning machinery like the Centre and State with the lower machinery like Panchayat Samiti at the block and Gram Panchayats at the grass root level.

THE STRUCTURE OF PANCHAYATI RAJ SYSTEM

Zilla Parishad
(At the District Level)

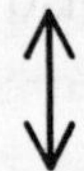

Panchayat Samiti
(At the Block Level)

Gram Panchayat
(At the Panchayat Level)

Village, Gram Sabha
(At the Village Level)

FINANCIAL INSTITUTION

In the rural areas, there is at present a wider spectrum of financial agencies directly or indirectly involved in Rural Development. These agencies mainly comprise of Co-operative banks, Commercial banks and Regional Rural Banks. All these institutions are again linked with apex institution like National Bank for Agriculture and Rural Development (NABARD) for refinancing and borrowing purposes. There is thus a multi-agency approach to rural financing engaged in rural development activities.

COOPERATIVES

The cooperative banking system was introduced in India in the year 1904 as a Credit movement to assist the farmers for higher agricultural production. In course of time, the Co-operative Credit institutions became inevitable and important institution for Rural Development.

The cooperative credit structure is broadly classified into two types. They are short-term and long-term credit co-operatives. The short-term cooperative credit structure is of three-tier system. This system is federal in nature and pyramidical in type. At the apex of the pyramid, there is the State Co-operative bank. There are Central Co-operative banks (CCBs) at the district or intermediate level. At the bottom, there is the Primary Agricultural Co-operative Credit Societies (PACs). They operate mostly at the village level. In recent years the Farmers Service Societies (FSS) and Large-sized Agricultural Multipurpose Co-operative Societies (LAMPS) have been added to the existing base level institutions. However, in the entire Co-operative Credit Structure, the Primary Cooperative Credit Societies occupy a strategic position on account of their direct links with the farmers and weaker section people at the grass root level. The long-term Credit Co-operative Structure is of two-tier system. There is Central Land Development Bank (CLDB) at the top and Primary Land Development Banks (PLDBs) at the base level.

The State Co-operative Bank is the apex bank in the short-term Co-operative Credit Structure. The area of operation of the bank is extended to the entire State. The management of the bank is vested in the board of Directors. The directors are the President/Chairman of the Central, Cooperative banks and Government Nominees like, the Registrar Co-operative Societies, the director of agriculture and Food Production and the director of Textiles. The Board appoints the Chief Executive Officer/The Managing Director/The General Manager for the day-to-day administration of the bank.

The Working Capital of the State Co-operative banks consists of share capital, reserve funds, deposits from members, direct State contribution and borrowings. The major part of the resources of SCBs mobilised through various sources is generally utilised for loans and advances to CCBs and PACs. Most of the loans advanced by SCBs is for seasonal agricultural operations. Loans are also advanced for Marketing of crops, industrial purposes, consumption purposes etc. The apex bank provides the link between the RBI/NABARD and the Money market on the one hand, and the entire Co-operative Credit Structure on the other. The SCBs, therefore occupies a key position in the entire structure of Short-term and Medium-term Co-operative Credit. The SCBs also issue guidelines to CCBs & PACs relating to advance of loans to special rural development programmes.

The position of Central Co-operative banks (CCBs) is of crucial importance in the Co-operative Credit Structure. They form an important link between the State Co-operative bank, at the apex and the PACs at the base.

The management of the CCB is vested with a board of Directors consisting of its members from different affiliated societies and the nominated members of the State Government. The CCBs obtain their funds through the share capital, deposits, membership fees, reserve funds, and borrowings from apex bank or refinance from the RBI/NABARD. The CCBs advance short-term loans to primary agricultural Co-operative Credit Societies for meeting current farm expenses and medium-term loans for land reclamation, building of cattle sheds, purchase of cattle and pump sets and construction and repairing of wells for irrigation purposes etc. These loans are granted on proper security such as landed assets, house mortgage, agricultural produce, gold or ornaments, fixed deposits, Life Insurance Policies, Government Promisory notes executed by the borrowing societies. They also advance loans to rural Development Programmes as per government norms and directives.

The last tier of the Co-operative banking structure is

Primary Agricultural Co-operative Societies (PACs). These societies have direct linkage with the farmers and they are purely operating in the rural areas. The village credit society is the best agency to inculcate the habit of thrift, self-help and mutual help among its members. It is engaged in securing for its members services of various kinds. It has to keep the concepts of mutuality and ethical dealings in mind and ensure sufficient social cohesion. The efficiency of the co-operative banking structure depends primarily upon the efficiency of the grass root level co-operative societies. "As a matter of fact; the PACs are the foundation on which the entire co-operative structure is built upon." The Primary Agricultural Credit Societies cover different types of Credit Societies, through the common feature of all these different societies is that most of their members are agriculturists. The group includes (1) Large-size societies that include rural banks, agricultural banks and credit unions (2) Service co-operatives and (3) other small size societies. More clearly, at present there exists Primary Agricultural Cooperative Credit Societies (PACs), Farmers Service Societies (FSS) and Large-sized Agricultural Multi-purpose Co-operative societies (LAMPs) at the village level. They form the Primary Cooperatives in most of the States.

A Co-operative Society can be formed by at least 10 members after due permission and registration by the registrar of Co-operative Societies. In the management of Society, its general body, consisting of all its members, is the supreme authority. The general body elects a managing committee or executive committee consisting of President or Chairman Secretary and other eight to nine members. The Secretary generally is the paid employee of the Society, where as all other members including the President or Chairman is honorary. The PACs obtain their funds in the form of deposits, membership fees, and borrowings from higher co-operative institutions. Normally, the members are eligible to borrow from the society. There is no scope of borrowing by the non-members. The societies have undertaken distribution of fertilizer and have arrangements to hire or supply agricultural implements including plant protection equipments. Some societies have been entrusted with the distribution of essential consumer goods under public distribution system. However, the PACs have mainly remained as credit dispensing agencies for the agriculturists in the rural areas. They play a very insignificant role in non-credit activities.

In order to overcome this problem Farmers Service Societies were established as a base level institution on the recommendation of National Commission on Agriculture in the year 1971. The important objective of FSS is to provide a package of inputs and consumer services along with Technical advice and supporting services like, storage, transportation, processing and marketing at a single contact point.

A board of directors manages the activities of the FSS. There are eleven members in the board. One fulltime paid director manages the day-to-day activities of FSS. Of the remaining 10 directors, five are the farmer members of the FSS; of whom three are small and marginal farmers and two are farmers of other categories. The remaining five directors are; a representative of the financing institution a Block Development Officer, an Assistant Director of Agriculture, an Assistant Director of Veterinary Services and an Assistant Registrar of Co-operative Societies.

The Funds of the FSS mobilised through the acceptance of deposits from its members. Beside the sponsoring bank extend financial assistance. The State Government also contributes towards its share capital.

The FSSs are meeting all the credit requirements of their members. The FSS advances short-term, medium-term and long-term loans. All this is undertaken as per the guidelines of the financing bank. Besides, the FSS take up the business for supplying various agricultural inputs and services at reasonable prices. The institution also deals with the marketing of products for their members. They also undertake the construction of wells, minor irrigation projects, godowns etc. for their members.

The Ministry of Agriculture appointed a committee on co-operative structure in tribal areas in 1971 under the

Chairmanship of Sri K.S.Bawa. Sri Bawa recommended the Organisation of Integrated Credit cum Marketing Co-operative Societies termed as Large-sized Agricultural Multi-purpose Co-operative Societies (LAMPs). This organisation generally operates in the tribal areas. This covers a block of ten villages. This is also expected to cover on an average 10 and 20 thousands population.

A board of directors manages the activities of the LAMPs. The board generally consists of eleven members. The Managing Director is the functional head of the organisation of the remaining 10 directors five are elected from among the tribal members. The other 5 directors belong to Financial Institutions, Block Development Officer, Co-operative Societies, Tribal department etc.

The Funds of the LAMPs are mobilised in the form of Share Capital, paid up capital, deposits and borrowings. The LAMPs provide short and medium-term agricultural loans, procures all major inputs and services and also buys produce of the tribal farmers. It also open consumer stores and act as retail that outlet of the State's public distribution system. Sometimes, the long-term loans are also sanctioned to eligible borrowers of the locality.

The long-term cooperative credit institutions needs of the agriculturists have catered the long-term credit. They are Central/State Land Development bank operate at the State level and Primary Land Development Banks (PLDBs) at the district/ sub-divisional level.

The Land Development banks, which are also known as land mortgage banks and agricultural development banks in some states made a beginning in the Nineteen hundred twenties. The long-term Co-operative Credit Structure, unlike the short-term structure is not uniform throughout the Country. The structural patterns of these banks are of three types, like;

(i) Federal Type: The usual federal type with the Central Land Development Bank (CLDB) at the top and the Primary Land Development Banks (PLDBs) at the base. This system prevails in the States like, Andhra Pradesh, Assam, Haryana, Kerala, Madhya Pradesh, Karnataka, Orissa, Punjab, Rajasthan, Tamil Nadu and West Bengal.

(ii) Unitary type: The CLDBs advancing loans direct to individuals operating through branches. The States not mentioned above adopted unitary type of long-term Credit Structure.

(iii) Mixed type: The CLDBs operating through branches as well as PLDBs. The membership of the CLDBs comprises of PLDBs, other co-operative banks and societies and individuals. The management of the bank is vested to a Board of Management elected as per provisions of the Act, Rules and Byelaws. The State Government also nominates the Directors for Board of Directors or Board of Management. The financial resource of the bank consists of the share capital from members, reserves created out of profits, borrowing, deposits, sales of debentures and refinancing from RBI/NABARD. The bank provides long-term productive credit through the PLDBs.

The Primary Land Development Banks (PLDBs) generally grant long-term loans to farmers for farm development activities. The area of operation of PLDBs differs from State to State. In some States, it extends to whole of a district while in others it extends to a sub-division or a few talukas. The General body of members is the Supreme authority of management of a PLDB. The general body elects the Board of Directors or Managing Committee. For day-to-day management, full time manager, secretary, accountant and other supporting staff are employed. In some of the States, the CLDBs have introduced Cadre Scheme, under which managers of PLDBs are recruited and trained by the CLDBs and posted to work in primaries affiliated to them.

The Funds of the bank is mobilised through share capital from members. The main part of the fund is mobilised through the borrowings from the apex bank, NABARD and from other agencies. It also obtains finance in the form of deposits, grants and subsidies etc. from the State Governments. Generally these banks advance loans to undertake farm activities in long-term basis. Usually, loans are granted on the first mortgage of land. In course of time they extend loan for off-farm activities like, marketing, transportation, etc.

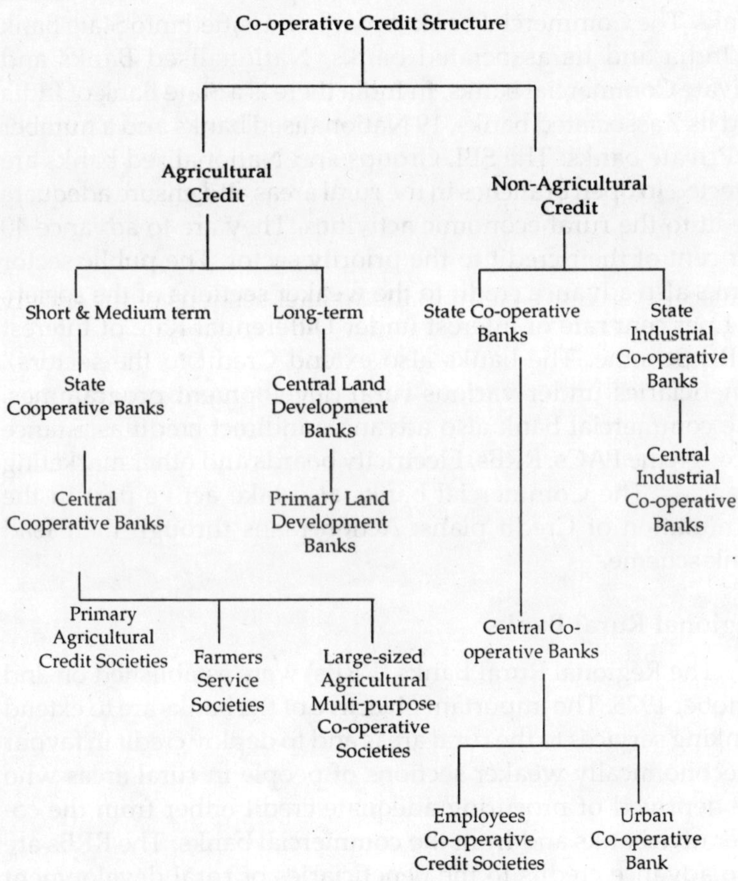

Besides, the Agricultural Credit Cooperatives. There is non-agricultural Cooperative operating in the rural areas. The weavers Cooperative Societies, Industrial Co-operative Societies working for the development of Village and cottage industries.

Whereas Consumers Cooperative Societies working for the consumers/general public for smooth functioning of public distribution systems.

Commercial Banks

In rural areas there are a wide spectrum of Commercial banks. The Commercial banks broadly classified into State Bank of India and its associated banks, Nationalised Banks and Private Commercial banks. In India there is a State Bank of India and its 7 associated banks, 19 Nationalised banks and a number of Private banks. The SBI, Groups and Nationalised banks are directed to open branches in the rural areas and ensure adequate credit to the rural economic activities. They are to advance 40 per cent of their credit to the priority sector. The public sector banks also advance credit to the weaker sections of the society at 4 per cent rate of interest under Differential Rate of Interest (DRI) Scheme. The banks also extend Credit to the sectors/ beneficiaries under various rural development programmes. The commercial bank also advances indirect credit assistance through the PACs, RRBs, Electricity boards and other marketing agencies. The Commercial banks also take active part in the formulation of Credit plans; Action plans through their lead bank scheme.

Regional Rural Banks

The Regional Rural Banks (RRBs) were established on 2nd October 1975. The important objective of the banks are to extend banking services to the rural areas and to deploy credit in favour of economically weaker sections of people in rural areas who are deprived of procuring adequate credit either from the co-operative banks and from the commercial banks. The RRBs are also advance credits to the beneficiaries of rural development programmes. The credit advanced by RRBs are short-term, medium-term and long-term in nature. Besides, they are required to provide indirect finance to Co-operative Societies and the farmers Service Societies operating within its area of operation. The banks also provide consumption loans within the specified limits.

The management of the RRBs vests with the board of directors comprises of a members. The Chairman of the banks generally belongs to the sponsored Nationalised bank. Three directors are nominated by the Central Government; two directors are nominated by the State Government the remaining five directors including the Chairman are nominated by the sponsoring bank. The Funds of the RRBs are mainly mobilised through share capital, contribution, deposits and borrowings. The funds so mobilised are generally channelised to meet the credit needs of the weaker sections.

NABARD

The Apex bank for agriculture and Rural Development is National Bank for Agriculture and Rural Development (NABARD). The Bank established in July 1982 after the recommendation of the Committee to Review Arrangements for Institutional Credit for Agriculture and Rural Development (CRAFICARD) headed by Sri B.Sivaraman. The Management of the NABARD is entrusted to a Board of Directors. The Board consists of 15 members, like; a Chairman, a Managing Director, 2 Experts in rural economics, 3 experts from Co-operative and Commercial banks, 3 Sitting Directors from the Board of RBI, 3 Directors from Government of India and 2 is nominated from amongst the State Government officials. NABARD formulate developmental policy, planning and operational matters relating to credit for agriculture and rural development. It provides refinance facilities to the Co-operative banks, Commercial banks and Regional Rural Banks. It issues guideline and inspect co-operative banks and the RRBs. The credit institutions operating at the grass root level also borrow Funds from NABARD. In India there exists the Multi-agency approach to rural financing. The basic and important philosophy of this approach is to ensure perfect coordination among all the Agencies operating in the rural areas for the common objective of meeting the credit needs of the rural economic activities along with the borrowers belong to weaker sections.

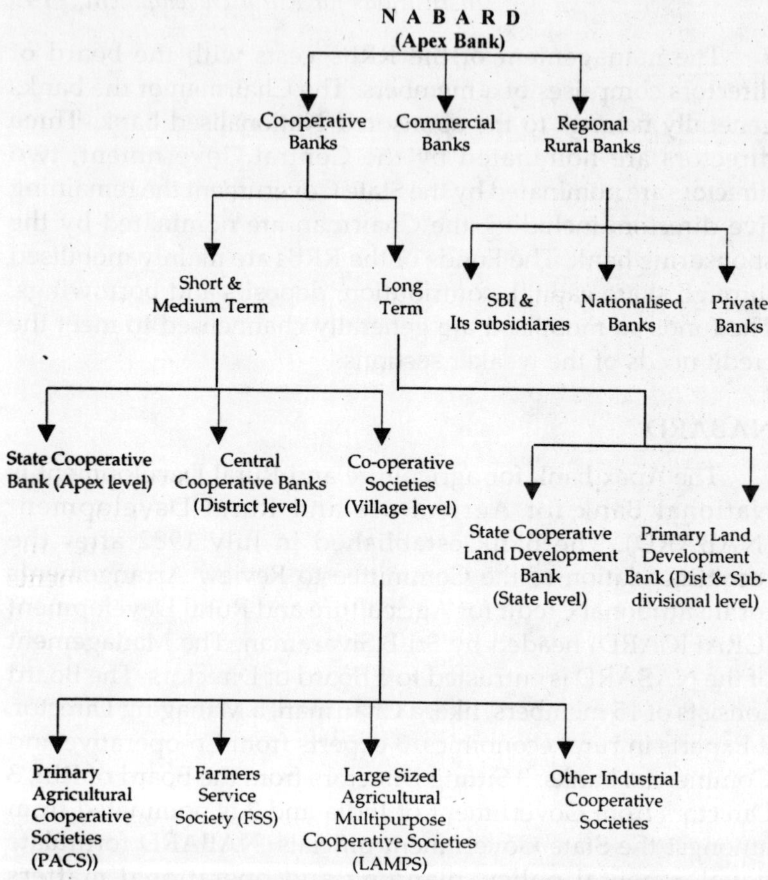
N A B A R D
(Apex Bank)
Co-operative Banks
Commercial Banks
Regional Rural Banks
Short & Medium Term
Long Term
SBI & Its subsidiaries
Nationalised Banks
Private Banks
State Cooperative Bank (Apex level)
Central Cooperative Banks (District level)
Co-operative Societies (Village level)
State Cooperative Land Development Bank (State level)
Primary Land Development Bank (Dist & Sub-divisional level)
Primary Agricultural Cooperative Societies (PACS))
Farmers Service Society (FSS)
Large Sized Agricultural Multipurpose Cooperative Societies (LAMPS)
Other Industrial Cooperative Societies

OBSERVATIONS, PROBLEMS AND SUGGESTIONS

India is an economically underdeveloped country. The condition of rural economy is worse. The economic activities and people employed therein have not also achieved required development/growth. In order to break the jinx of rural economic sector, Government through its different plans introduced a number of rural development programmes. The programmes are also varied in nature. They are of sector, area and target oriented programmes. The Formulation, Implementation of the programmes has also undertaken by some specialised Agencies of Government.

In addition the NGOs, the Panchayati Raj institutions, financial institutions involved themselves in the success of the programmes. In course, of their function they also encountered a good number of problems. The problems were also varied in nature. As the book/based on the macro level information/data. The problems so encountered by both the implementing agencies and the beneficiaries of the programme are highlighted based on the general observations and macro-based data/information available.

The problems mainly highlights the problems encountered by the Government as the planning and implementing machinery the Associated/ancillary agencies inevitable for the fruitful implementation of such rural development programmes, they are the Rural Development agencies/institutions/ Departments, Financial Institutions, Non-

Governmental Organisations, working as intermediary agencies for the implementation of rural development programmes/ schemes. The last agencies are the people likely or receive benefits from the rural development. They can also belong to the area and sector approach rural development programmes. Thus, we can classify the rural development agency into three as; Government, Intermediary/Ancillary agencies and the targeted people/beneficiaries. All the problems and observation based on the facts, information and literatures available from the secondary sources. These may not hold good in all respects.

(1) More Generalised Programme

Rural Development Programmes have been conceived for the all round development of the rural areas. However, the rural development programmes are launched in the context of general problems of the rural areas. It fails to give importance to some particular and area issues. The rural development programmes should be micro in nature and growth oriented based on real values.

(2) Inadequate Coordination

As per the Guidelines all the developmental programmes in the rural areas are to be planned/formulated by the DRDA in cooperation and coordination of other departments and financial institution, agencies of peoples representatives etc. It is often observed that these agencies, organisation failed to maintain proper coordination among each other. All the agencies/organisations are trying their best to stick to their own principles and ideologies. In the process cooperation and coordination are not maintained. The Agencies responsible for the formulation, Implementation and evaluation of the Rural Development Programme is required to maintaining good co-ordination among them.

(3) Based on Ruling Party Principles and Ideologies

In India, the rural development programmes are conceived/launched as per the principles and ideologies of the ruling party. Besides, in the participation for planning, formulation and implementation through their representatives tried to maintain such principles and ideologies. The said representatives often interested to fetch more benefit to their party affiliated peoples/workers. This does not cover the problems of all class people. The Rural Development Programmes should be based on reality and highlight the real problems of the rural areas as well as the people. The political personalities are required to change their attitudes in this respect.

(4) Inadequate Funds

The rural development programmes require more capital investment. The Economic Sectors of rural areas remain more or less traditional. These sectors also adopt traditional methods of production. In order to attain rural development the transformation of technologies is required. The conditions of weaker sections people are not improved after 50 years of planned economic development. The upliftment of their socio-economic condition also require high dose of investment. In our country, a fixed amount of funds are allocated for a particular rural development Programme. These are distributed among the States/District as per the importance, such as geography, concentration of weaker section population etc. The share of the Fund to cope with the local problems seems to be inadequate. Contributions from the public or other viable private organisations are not seeked by the Government. Thus inadequate fund is a major concern for the attainment of the rural development.

(5) Land based Economy

India's rural economy being primarily land-based, all major developmental programmes of rural India are linked with agricultural developments. It is also evident that most of the available resources are controlled by few, this reinforces the hegemony of the few over many and the benefits do not tickle down to those who need them most. Besides, the precarious land and man ratio suggests that by introducing radical land redistribution in rural India very limited egalitarian goals can be achieved and if done so, that will mean only sharing of poverty and no real development.

(6) Authority Structure

Rural development plan implementation is required to be accepted by the local level functionaries who attend the District consultative committee meetings and that they are in a position to mobilise financial and organisational resources to fulfill accepted commitments. It is observed that the authority structure in the administration and the banks is such that those who attend such meetings are neither in a position to accept firm commitments on behalf of their departments, banks without reference to higher authorities not to act accordingly. Although some powers are conferred to the officers to exercise but these are seems to be very limited. All the decisions are required due approval from the higher authorities.

(7) Leakage of benefits

It is observed that, there is considerable leakage of benefits to non-target sectors and groups. Most of the rural development programmes are conceived to improve the Socio-Economic condition of the weaker sections like small, marginal farmers, agricultural and non-agricultural labourers, rural artisans, scheduled castes, scheduled tribes and deprived women etc. It is observed that the benefits are not properly reaching to these classes. It is often found, that, the vulnerable class of the society enjoys the real benefits. The subsidy components of the rural development programmes tend to allow to non-target groups, specially the programme implementing bureaucratic class, rather than including expansion of production base of the beneficiaries. Due to illiteracy and ignorance the real benefits sometimes enjoyed by the Third party commonly speaking the middlemen and the village touts including the petty personnel having a little political affiliation.

(8) Low Sustaining Impact

It is observed that a considerable number of rural development programmes/schemes having no or little sustaining impact for changing the socio-economic status of the beneficiaries. The assets created from the credit assistance of financial institutions and subsidies of the development/ administrative agencies are short lived (Particularly incase of livestock assets) failed to push the beneficiaries up on the scale of production and productivity. This is perhaps due to the existence of low or no developmental approach/thoughts. This factor again dominated by the lack of awareness about the programmes.

(9) Dominance of welfare over productivity

In India, most of the rural development programmes are based on the basic welfare principles. These schemes are backed by both credit and subsidy components. Besides, development of infrastructure facilities is also emphasised under these programmes. It is also evident that provision of long-term credit and based on the principle of write off by political parties also have adverse effect on the productivity of economic sectors. It is observed that the subsidy component is often extending up to 100 per cent in some selected schemes and class of beneficiaries. This reduces the productive motive, attitude of the beneficiaries.

(10) Based on the principles and policies of political parties

In our country most of the rural development programmes are either based on the principles of the political parties or biased by their ideologies. Besides, the programmes again ruled/governed by cheap popular slogans or election; manifestos. Due to these, causes the programmes failed to attain the expected success. It is also observed that after the completion of one political party's rule the next political party, which assumes power, hesitates to carry out the same. Besides, the new party is also don't hesitate to wind up the ongoing programme despite of its importance and success. In India, due to these problems, the rural development has not attained after five decades of the planned economic development.

SUGGESTIONS

- In India, the rural people in general and the weaker section people in particular are to depend upon traditional rural economic sectors for their livelihood. The rate of literacy in rural areas is very low in comparison to urban areas. Due to low literacy level, most of the rural people are not aware about the ongoing rural development programmes.

  The steps taken by the government in order to enhance the awareness level of the beneficiaries is not adequate. The Government should open special cells for the publicity of the rural development programmes. The Government is required to adopt the publicity method, which is conducive to the nature and requirement of the rural people. The people are to be provided with adequate instruments for enhancement of awareness level. The existing system of publicity about the rural development is required to be re-considered and should be based on rural realities prior to the Selection of the Scheme as well as the Beneficiaries, the implementing agencies should provide details of the programme to the rural people, who are likely to be benefitted serious endeavour is, therefore, needed to make the rural people aware about the resources earmarked for rural development in various Government departments.

- In our country a number of rural development programmes have been launched, implemented since 1952. It is often said that, the rural development programmes failed to attain its desired goal due to improper identification of the programmes, schemes and the beneficiaries therein. The Implementing

Agencies attitude to implement the programme is target oriented. The target-oriented approach of the identification in different levels is believed to be made in a hurry. This approach forced the agencies for wrong identification of programmes, schemes and beneficiaries. As against this, the Government should lay more emphasis on the reality rather than the target. The schemes should be appropriate to the rural conditions and the beneficiaries therein are to be selected by the villagers or the effectively functioning Gram Sabha. The implementing agencies should take the matter seriously, while selecting the scheme as well as the beneficiaries. The selection of the schemes is needed to be made by the beneficiaries. Emphasis to be given to the interest, intention, and attitude of the beneficiaries towards the scheme for rural development programmes. It is to conclude that, A realistic programme on rural development with the potentiality of the successful implementation, can only be prepared if rural poor are taken into confidence and are assisted to draw the development programme, taking the village as unit. Outsiders, as technocrats, Economists etc. should only assist them as Friends to make their own decision.

- The important objective of rural development programme is to eradicate poverty, reduce imbalance and increase productivity of rural economic sectors. Thus, the beneficiaries of rural development programmes are rural poor living below the poverty line. The poverty line in India determined by the relative standards. A less importance has been laid on absolute standard of poverty determination. Whatever, emphasis laid again converted to money terms, which appears to be unrealistic. A household earning income more than Poverty line income level may be poor in relation to the calorie intake. Thus, the determination of poverty line required re-considered. Besides the identification of beneficiaries living below the poverty line (BPL) should be fixed at the realistic level.

- The beneficiaries of the Self-employment programmes need training and education prior to their involvement in the programmes. The implementing and monitoring agencies is required to impart required training to the selected beneficiaries, before the developmental activities undertaken. Besides, rural people should be provided with the scope of expressing their own felt needs and need to be provided with an opportunity to choose economic activities for their own development.
- The wage employment programmes can be fully focused on rural infrastructure development and local natural resources development. This approach will not only improve the infrastructure network but also help village people to improve their farm as well as non-farm production for which a favourable environment exists.
- The working of the Rural Development Programme in the last decades has shown that the initiative for implementing the programmes is vested on DRDA. The role of DRDA is more or less confined to the planning and release of subsidies for rural development programmes. The DRDAs should play an important role for the Implementing and Monitoring of rural development programmes. Regular monitoring and evaluation of rural development programmes in real manner could solve the ongoing problems encountered therein and can also helpful to solve the problems. This will pave the path of success to the rural development programmes and attainment of rural development.
- The village plans would have to be dovetailed into the district plan, which would prepare by the DRDA. Proper appraisal of the rural development schemes is needed. Besides, for the success of Rural

Development Programmes it should be ensured that the Project Directors of the DRDA are given tenure of not less than three years so as to inculcate in them a sense of commitment to the programme. The other staff in the key posts should not be disturbed frequently.

- The various Government departments with specialised expertise and banks should work in close co-operation with the district planning unit in order to have a coordinated and scientific plan, the availability of local resources, the potential for alternative productive works and of viable schemes, to be looked into.
- Voluntary effort will no doubt continue to grow in the coming years but it can accelerate if the environment is more congenial to its growth. Voluntary Organisations with professional and Managerial Capabilities can act as a catalyst and can organise beneficiaries, involve people in planning and development and provide the necessary support to make development a reality. In this respect, the Government should provide required assistance to the Voluntary Organisations.
- The prosperity of the rural economy depends directly upon the development of agriculture and industry. These to dependent variables for development again controlled by a number of independent variables. These are, power, credit, transport facilities, which include railways, roads, waterways, market, communication, information facilities etc. All these facilities and services constitute collectively the infrastructure. The development and expansion of these facilities are an essential pre-condition for attainment of economic development and rural development. "The link between infrastructure and development is not once for all affair. It is a continuous process and progress in development has to be

preceded, accompanied and followed by progress in infrastructure, if we are to fulfill our declared objectives of a self-accelerating process of economic development. Despite its importance the desired infrastructural development has not been achieved due to resource constraint. In view of the resource constraint, further expansion of facilities may be secured by a shift of priority from high cost technology to low cost technology, from public funding to private financing and from large-scale public management to small-scale private/co-operative/community management in appropriate areas required for rural development.

- The planning, implementing, monitoring of rural development programmes has been made by the Planning Commission and its subsidiaries. In the process they have been facing a number of difficulties. Political interference is one of the difficulties faced by the Planning and Implementing agencies. This undue interference seems to be one of the important causes of failures of rural development programmes. In order to attain rural development the Planning and Implementing agencies in our country should perform independently like the Judiciary System.

SELECT BIBILIOGRAPHY

Adarkar, B.N., *Commercial Banks in India After Nationalisation*, A.D. Shroff Memorial Trust, Bombay, 1971.

Adelman, Irma & et al., *Economic Growth and Social Equity in Developing Countries*, Stanford University Press, Stanford, California, 1973.

Angaria, J.J., *Essays in Planning and Growth*, Vora & Co., Publishers, Bombay, 1972.

Bhattacharya, S., *Rural Development in India and Developing Countries*, Metropolitan Book Co. Pvt. Ltd., New Delhi, 1983.

Brahmananda, P.R. and Panchamukhi, V.R. (Ed), *The Development Process in the Indian Economy*, Himalaya Publishing House, New Delhi, 1987.

Brahmananda, P.R., *Planning for a Futureless Economy*, Himalaya Publishing House, Bombay, 1978.

Chambers, Roberts, *Rural Development, Putting the Last First*, Longman, London, 1985.

Chandrasekhar, C.P., *India's Economic Development, Development for Whom?* Chennai Book House, Madras, 1979.

Chaturvedi, T.N.(Ed) *Rural Development: Some Themes and Dimensions*, Indian Institute of Public Administration, New Delhi, 1986.

Cheema, G. Shabbir (Ed), *Rural Development in Asia*, Sterling Publishers Pvt. Ltd., New Delhi, 1985.

Dantwalla, M.L., *Poverty in India, Then and Now* (1870-1970), Macmillan, India, 1973

________________*Asian Seminar on Rural Development: the Indian Experience*, Oxford & IBH Publishing Co. Pvt. Ltd., New Delhi, 1986.

Deb, K., *Rural Development in India since Independence*, Sterling Publishers Pvt. Ltd., New Delhi, 1986.

Desai, P.B., *Planning in India*, Vikash Publishing House, New Delhi, 1979.

Desai, Vasant, *A Study of Rural Economics*, Himalaya Publishing House, Bombay, 1983.

________________*Rural Development* (Vol.I to VI), Himalaya Publishing House, Bombay, 1988.

Durdy, P.J. (Ed), *Regional and Rural Development - Essays in Theory and Practice*, Alpha Academic, Great Britain, 1976.

Dutta, A.A. (Ed), *India: Resources, Potentialities and Planning*, IBH Publishing Co, Oxford and IBH, New Delhi, 1975.

Franda, Marcus, *India's Rural Development*, Indiana University Press, London, 1979.

Gadgil, D.R., *Planning and Economic Policy in India*, Gokhale Institute of Politics and Economics, Poona, 1972.

Ghatak, Subrata, *Rural Money Markets in India*, Macmillan Company of India Ltd., 1976.

Gupta, S.C., *Development Banking for Rural Development*, Deep & Deep Publication New Delhi - 1987.

Hunter, Guy, *Integrated Rural Development Approach, Strategy and Perspectives*, Abhinav Publications, New Delhi, 1977.

Hye, Hasnat Abdul, *Integrated Approaches to Rural Development*, Sterling Publishers Pvt. Ltd., New Delhi, 1986.

Jain, S.C., *Rural Development-Institutions and Strategies*, Rawat Publications, Jaipur, 1985.

Jha, L.K., *Economic Development - Ends and Means*, Vora & Co., Bombay, 1973.

Krishen, Thorkil, *Development in Rich and Poor Countries*, Praeger Publishers, New York, 1982.

Krishnamachari, V.T. & Venue, S., *Planning in India, Theory and Practice*, Orient Longmans, Bombay, 1977.

Kurien, C.T., *Poverty, Planning and Social Transformation*, Allied Publishers, Bombay, 1978.

Lahiri, T.B., *Rural Development, a short-term strategy*, Jayashree Prakashan, Calcutta, 1980.

Lea, David, A.M. and Choudhury, D.P., *Rural Development and the State*, Mathuen & Co., London, 1983.

Lewis, W.A., *Principles of Planning*, George Allen & Unwin, London, 1960.

Maheswari, Sriram, *Rural Development in India—A Public Policy Approach*, Sage Publications, New Delhi, 1985.

Mathew, T. (Ed), *Rural Development in India*, Agricole Publishing Academy, New Delhi, 1984.

Meheta, Shiv R., *Rural Development: Policies and Programmes*, Sage Publications, New Delhi, 1984.

Misra, Bidyadhar et. al. (Ed), *Economic Development of Orissa*, Vidyapuri, Cuttack, 1991.

Misra, S.N. and Sahu, B.K., *Multi-Agency System and Rural Development in India*, Spellbound Publications Pvt. Ltd.; Rohtak, 1997.

Mishra, R.P. and Sunderam, K.V., *Rural Area Development Perspectives and Approach*, Sterling Publications Pvt. Ltd., New Delhi, 1979.

Mishra, Madhu S., (Ed) *Rural Development in Eastern and North-*

Eastrn India, Publications Division, Indian Institute of Management, Calcutta, 1988.

Nakkiran, S., *Co-operative Banking in India*, Rainbow Publications, Coimbatore, 1980.

National Institute of Community Development, *Awareness of Community Development in Village India*, Hyderabad, 1967.

National Institute of Rural Development, *Rural Development in India, Some Facets*, Hyderabad, 1981.

__________, *Rural Development Statistics*, Hyderabad, 1999.

Parthasarathy, G, "Reorientation of Rural Development Programmes, A note on some basic Issues," *Economic and Political Weekly* Vol.XX, No.48, Nov, 30, 1985.

Prasad, K.N., *India's Rural Problems*, Concept Publishing Co., New Delhi,1991.

Randhawa, M.S., *Developing Village India*, Orient Longman Ltd; Bombay, 1951.

Rastogi, P.N., *India's Rural Futures, Some Policy Issues*, Centre for Policy Research, New Delhi, 1979.

Rath, Nilakantha, "Garibi Hatao: Can IRDP Do it ?" *Economic & Political Weekly*, Vol.XX, No.6, Feb, 9, 1985.

Roy, Amal & et al., *Studies in Rural Development and Administration*, The World Press Pvt. Ltd., Calcutta, 1984.

Saurath, Vivek, *Dynamics of Rural Development* (Vol.I to Vol.III), Dominant Publishers & Distributors, New Delhi, 1999.

Setty, E.D., *New Approaches to Rural Development*, Anmol Publications Pvt. Ltd., New Delhi, 2002.

Sharma, D.P. and Desai, V.V., *Rural Economy of India*, Vikash Publishing House Pvt. Ltd., Ghaziabad, 1980.

Sharma, S.K. & et al., *Integrated Rural Development: Appraoch Strategy and Perspectives*, Abhinav Publications, New Delhi, 1977.

Singh, R.P., *Sociology of Rural Development in India*, Discovery Publishing House, New Delhi, 1987.

Srinivasan, E.S., *Financial Structure and Economic Development*, Sterling Publishers Pvt. Ltd., New Delhi, 1977.

Subramanya, S. (Ed), *Trends and Progress of Banking in India*, Deep and Deep Publications, N.Delhi, 1986.

Tewari, R.I. and Sinha, R.C., *Rural Development in India*, Ashish Publishing House, New Delhi, 1985.

Tripathy, S., *Development for Rural Poor*, Rawat Publications, Jaipur, 1987.

Wadhwa, C.D., *Rural Banks for Rural Development*, Macmillan, Madras, 1980.

(B) Govt. Publications

Govt. of India

National Cooperative Development Corporation (Ministry of Agriculture), Summary Report of the Study Team on Corporative Credit Structure, New Delhi, 1974.

Planning Commission, Various Five Year Plans, New Delhi, (First Five Year Plan to Eighth Five Year Plan).

Planning Commission, Interim Report on IADP in Canal irrigated areas by the task force on IRD, New Delhi, 1972.

RBI, Report of the All-India Rural Credit Review Committee (Chairman B.Venkartappiah), Bombay, 1969.

Census of India (Relevant Issues).

Govt. of Orissa

Department of Agriculture & Cooperation Agricultural Credit Projects—Banking Plan (Orissa), 1976.

Department of Planning and Coordination, various Five Year Plans. (First Five Year Plan to Eighth Five Year Plan) Orissa.

________________ *Economic Survey* (Relevant Issues).

Registrar of Cooperative Societies, Co-operative Movement in Orissa, (Relevant Issues).

INDEX

□□□